"Words of Encouragement &

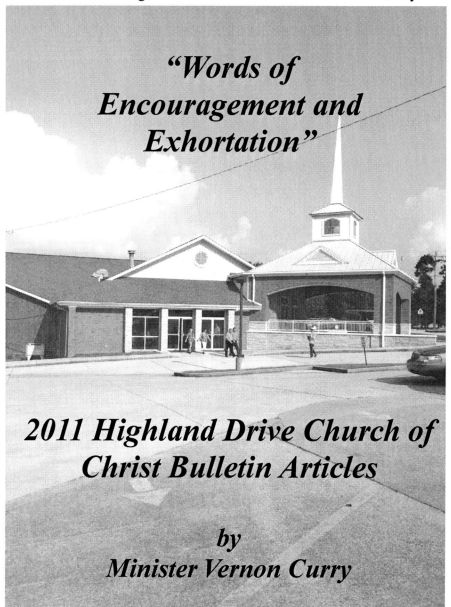

"Words of Encouragement and Exhortation"

2011 Highland Drive Church of Christ Bulletin Articles

by
Minister Vernon Curry

Dedications

Words of Encouragement and Exhortation – 2011 Highland Drive Church of Christ Bulletin Articles is dedicated to my wife, Judy Curry.

Judy through her understanding and patience has made it possible for me to do the work of preaching the Word.

She has walked the Christian life with me for over forty years. Thank you, Judy for walking by my side!

Author Auto-Bio

I was born in Poplar Bluff, Missouri, to Isaac and Myrtle Curry, and spent my childhood on a farm south of Fisk, Missouri, in the Depoyster community. I attended grade school in Depoyster the first five years of school, then went to Fisk-Rombauer and graduated from High School there.

I graduated from Abilene Christian College (now University) with a degree in Practical Bible. This was an additional four years of my spiritual training, which actually began in my parents' home when I was a baby. When I was two years old, some of the Christians in Depoyster had the vision and wisdom to start a Church of Christ in the community. I attended there until I went to college at the age of nineteen.

The first Sunday School Teacher that I remember was Mildred Turner who used card lessons to teach the little children. As I moved to older bible classes at Depoyster, we did not have bible class study books, but used only the Bible.

I began preaching at Depoyster during the summer of 1967. I look back with gratitude to the congregation for permitting me to begin to learn to preach. I have learned through the years that your education is never finished in gaining Bible knowledge, and on how to preach and teach the Word of God. I attended the Depoyster Church of Christ until I started college at Abilene Christian College at the age of nineteen

After college, I began preaching in Woodlake, California, then preached in various places in Missouri, Oklahoma, and Texas, many times working secular jobs to help support my family. The last several years, I have preached and worked with the good Christians of the Highland Drive Church of Christ in Poplar Bluff, Missouri serving as their fulltime pulpit minister and missionary to India.

In 1971, I was married to Judy Stout Gilley. We have four children and ten grandchildren.

In 2002, I made my first mission trip to India with Brother Don Eubanks. My second trip was in 2004 with my brother, Wayne Curry, and we have been back each year since with different members of the church. Most of the trips have been made with family members, with the exception of Don Eubanks, Don Barr, and Freda Lancaster, friend and fellow member at Highland.

Sharing the Gospel of Jesus Christ with non-Christians in India, and working with the fellow Christians in India has been a source of great joy.

I am forever grateful for all the Christian friends and family members who have influenced me walk the Christian life and encouraged me to preach the Gospel of my Lord and Savior Jesus Christ.

In Christian Love,

Vernon Curry

Vernon Curry

Minister
Highland Drive Church of Christ

Introduction

This collection of 2011 articles, ***Words of Encouragement and Exhortation – Volume II*** from the Highland Drive Church of Christ Bulletin, were written with the desire to teach, to encourage, and comfort my fellow Christians at Highland Drive Church of Christ in Poplar Bluff, MO. One of our four elders, Tom Carter, believed the articles were worth putting into book form and would be edifying and encouraging to a broader audience of Christians and non-Christians. I have given over to his wisdom.

The articles cover a variety of subjects. They have been organized by the date they were written. The table of contents gives the subject, date, and page number for each article.

Most of the topics are discussed for only one week. However, there are a few topics, which are continued into the next week.

I hope these articles will teach, inspire and comfort. I pray that you will receive the articles with graciousness. Any mistakes are the author's. In writing the articles, I have relied on my bible knowledge and personal experience that I have gained through the years. The articles are my writings, but I have been diligent to give credit to the many people who have influenced me and to reference quotes when possible.

In Christian Love,
Vernon

Copyright 2013
By author Vernon Curry
Edited by Thomas H. Carter, Ph.D.

All rights reserved.
No part of this publication may be reproduced, stored in a retrieval system or transmitted in any form or by any means, electronic, mechanical, photocopying, recording, or otherwise without the written permission of the publisher.

ISBN: 978-1-304-57504-3

Published 2013
Carter *Publishing*
2726 North10th Street
Poplar Bluff, Missouri 63901

Printed by lulu.com

Table of Contents

Topic	Date	Page No.
Dedications...		3
Author...		4
Minister Photo..		6
Introduction...		7
New Year's Resolutions........	01-02-11...............	11
Great Anticipation!................	01-09-11..............	13
The Journey......................	01-16-11..............	15
Ladders.............................	01-23-11..............	17
Mountain Experience..........	01-30-11..............	19
Some Things Never Change...	02-06-11..............	21
A Special Day.....................	02-13-11..............	23
What Use Is It?.....................	02-20-11..............	25
Favorite Songs....................	02-27-11..............	27
Discipline For Good............	03-06-11..............	29
A Convenient Time..............	03-13-11..............	31
Ambitious For the Lord........	03-20-11..............	33
Productive Christians...........	03-27-11..............	35
Enjoy the Trip.....................	04-03-11..............	37
Silence.............................	04-10-11..............	39
Preach the Word..................	04-17-11..............	41
How to Shake the Past!..........	05-01-11..............	43
How to Shake the Past-.........	05-08-11..............	45
You Shall Surely Die.............	05-15-01..............	47
My Want List.....................	05-22-11..............	49
Confrontation.....................	05-22-11..............	49
Live Like Jesus...................	05-22-11..............	50
The Church.......................	05-29-11.............,	51

"Words of Encouragement & Exhortation – 2011"   Curry

The End is Near!.................... 06-05-11............. 53
The Pressure of Life.............. 06-12-11............. 55
What to Look for in A Church... 06-19-11............. 57
A Legend Was In Our Town..... 06-26-11............. 59
You Can Do Mission Work.......07-03-11............. 61
You Can't Change the Past.......07-10-11............. 63
A Trip............................. 07-17-11............. 65
Teach the Gospel..................07-24-11............. 67
Vacation Bible School.............07-31-11............. 69
Hear the Word of God.............07-31-11............. 70
Two Brothers..................... 08-07-11............. 71
Walk With the Lord............... 08-14-11............. 73
The White of An Egg............., 08-21-11............. 75
In Order.......................... 08-29-11............. 77
Labor Day........................ 09-04-11............. 79
Its Not Anything!................. 09-11-11............. 81
It is Simple....................... 09-18-11............. 83
Salvation or Service.............. 09-25-11............. 85
Fear of the Lord.................. 10-02-11............. 87
Resurrection..................... 10-09-11............. 89
Quarrels.......................... 10-16-11............. 91
Working Together................10-23-11............. 93
Fellowship....................... 10-30-11..........,, 95
Thank You.......................11-20-11............. 97
Holidays......................... 11-20-11............. 97
Bible Reading, Prayer, & Love...11-20-11............. 98
What Is So Hard?................ 11-27-11............. 99
Two Sparrows...................12-04-11............. 101
What Matters?................... 12-04-11............. 102
Is It A State of Mind?............ 12-11-11............. 103
Frigidaire........................12-18-11............. 105
Paper............................12-25-11............. 107
Closing Thoughts................................. 109

10

2011 New Year's resolutions --

So many people tell me they do not keep New Year's Resolutions, so they have stopped making them. Is that the same as saying I give up? Do you believe you can improve yourself? I believe everyone can improve. I suggest some New Year's Resolutions.

Plan your spending. We all need to live within our income. For those who are older and have saved for their old age, it may be time to spend some of the money you saved for old age! It isn't bad or wrong to spend your savings when it reaches the time you have planned to spend it. Our spending needs to include helping those who are in need. So often we do not help others because we do not believe such to be in need. God says in **Ephesians 4:28:** *"Let him who stole steal no longer, but rather let him labor, working with his hands the thing which is good, that he may have something to give him who has need."* So often we readily agree with the first part of the verse, but choose to ignore the last part. Plan to obey God!

Plan your time. We all have the same number of hours in a day. Most of us will procrastinate every day. We do not plan our time. We practice putting off until tomorrow what doesn't have to be done today. God does not call us and demand that we read his word or else. He has told us the importance of the Bible. That is all we need to motivate us to use our time reading and meditating on the Bible. *"Redeeming the time, because the days are evil. Therefore do not be unwise, but understand what the will of the Lord is"* (**Ephesians 5:16-17**). If you have average intelligence, you can obey God. Where you spend eternity may very well depend on your use of your time.

Plan your reading of the Bible. Make it important enough in your life that you do it regularly. A man was planning to retire. I asked him what he would do. He said he did not know except he intended to keep reading the Bible everyday. It has been a few years since his retirement and he has continued to read daily. Don't just let the Bible fall open and read. Plan your reading. You may wish to read so many chapters per day or you may wish to spend a certain amount of time studying. You need to do what is best for you in studying the Bible!

Give yourself to exhortation. We study the Bible for our benefit. We study the Bible so we will be able to help others grow spiritually. We must know the Bible to be able to help others as well as ourselves. It is possible to know the Bible very well and neglect to exhort others to live a Christian life. The Bible gives us the plan of salvation. **The Bible gives us the correct way to worship God according to truth. The Bible gives us the right morals to live by.** We must learn the way of godliness. Others must be taught and encouraged to live godly lives. *"But exhort one another daily, while it is called 'today,' lest any of you be hardened through the deceitfulness of sin"* (**Hebrews 3:13**).

Humble yourself in obedience to the Lord. The obedience to the Lord starts from the heart! These two passages come to mind. *"But God be thanked that though you were slaves of sin, yet you obeyed from the heart that form of doctrine to which you were delivered"* (**Romans 6:17**). *"That if you confess with your mouth the Lord Jesus and believe in your heart that God has raised Him from the dead, you will be saved. For with the heart one believes unto righteousness, and with the mouth confession is made unto salvation"* (**Romans 10:9-10**). We must resolve to obey God, not our pride or any of man's ways!

Your life can be whatever you wish to make it. You can become the light for God in the world if you will do what God says!

Happy New Year!

Love, Vernon
01-02-11

Great Anticipation!

Life is full of opportunities for Christians. There are five people going from Missouri to India to teach and preach the gospel. It is exciting to be going for the ninth time. I did not know when I was invited the first time that I would go back several times.

I am writing this on Tuesday. We who are traveling must take malaria pills today. So I called all and reminded them. I then called Wayne and said I couldn't find my pills so he brought us some.

Dan is making his second trip. He has kept in touch by computer with some of the Christians whom he met last year. He has learned a few words of Telugu. He has prepared some special lessons for the trip. He, as all the rest, is leaving some family behind -- both his children are now attending Freed-Hardeman. He is leaving his wife and mother-in-law at his home.

Lil Warren is making her first trip. I am happy she going with us. Her enthusiasm is catching! She is nervous and excited at the same time. She knows more about India than I did my first trip. I had not seen pictures as we show. I did not know what lessons to teach. Lil has the opportunity to travel with four other Christians who have all been there. It will be a thrilling experience for her. She will be able to tell people about it for many years!

Judy is making her third trip. She does better physically in India, partly because of the climate, partly because she is away from the everyday stress of life. She has friends she is looking forward to seeing. The India women are very friendly, some very outgoing, some very shy. Judy, Freda and Lil have several lessons to choose from for teaching the women. I am happy to have Judy with me. She encourages me all the time, here or in India. We have many memories of our life together. We hope to grow old together and will have memories to share even about mission work.

Freda is also making her third trip. She is really admired by the women because of her age and dedication to the Lord. She has been studying her lessons, making candy which she gives to some friends in India. She, like all of us, has a list of things to take. She has been gathering other gifts for a few women. She, like many of us, must see the doctor before we go for refills of medicines. We must be sure we have enough medicines.

We thank all who have given. Congregations and individuals have given amounts from $10 to $2,000. Contributions have come from several states and many individuals and congregations. Each gift is important. We can go because you will send us. It would not be possible for us to make the trip without your contributions. We have more than necessary for our expenses. All of the money will be spent in India. Since we raise money for the India mission to carry them through the year, there is never too much.

I want to thank the Highland Drive Church of Christ for letting me go, even encouraging me to go. This is one of the most fruitful mission countries in the world now. The state we go to has about 75 million people. Many still have not heard the truth. Two years ago, a woman in the audience said that was the first sermon she had ever heard about Jesus! She asked for special prayer for her that she might know the truth.

We expect many baptisms, but only the Lord knows if there will be. We will speak in many congregations so they will be encouraged. All new Christians will be in contact with the local church even before they are baptized.

We ask for your prayers. **God is God**. We are his servants and your brothers and sisters in the church. We look forward to the next life where we hope to all spend eternity with God.

Love, Vernon
01-09-11

The Journey~

Many people want to enjoy the bliss of heaven. So many people are not enjoying the journey to heaven. **This life is the only journey we will make!** All will be judged following this life. There are only two places prepared for our souls to spend eternity – heaven or hell. I want to encourage you to enjoy the journey here on earth on your way to heaven. **We rejoice when one person is baptized into Jesus.** When one is baptized, their sins are taken away by God. The same event lets the Lord add that one person to the church. Baptism is just the beginning of the Christian life. This life is a happy one. We begin to walk with the Lord. Think, if you will, about the journey. **Being a Christian does not prevent one from sickness, heartache and death.** Being a Christian gives you a companion (God) to be with you while all these things are happening. The companionship of God brings peace which surpasses all understanding (**Philippians 4:7**). **When Christians face any crisis in their life, God is always there.** Some know what it is like to be alone in life. God is the strongest being. When one is on God's side, there is no one who can overcome that person. God is the companion of Christians.

There is *joy* as we start our journey from birth (baptism) to heaven. There is great joy in being born into the family of God! God takes away our sins. We are pure and holy in His sight. The guilt that we have lived with in the past is gone. There is no guilt because God has forgiven us! That is a great way to start the journey toward heaven.

It is a happy time when God talks with us! God talks with us as we travel along. He tells us when we are going the wrong way! He tells us when we are going the right way. He tells us with whom

"Words of Encouragement & Exhortation – 2011"   Curry

we are to be close companions. He tells us how to be forgiven of any sins we commit after we are baptized. He tells us that he loves us. He tells us of the reward which is waiting for us! All of these ideas are contained in the Bible. We can read it every day, and anytime we wish to hear God talk, we can read the Bible!

<u>Enjoy</u> **<u>God's companionship as he shares our happiness and our heartaches.</u>** He knows us better than we know ourselves. He loves us more than we love ourselves. We can speak to him any time. We can tell him about the problems which we have! Everyone has problems. Each day we need to take the time to talk with God. I use the word with, because we listen as we read the Bible and speak to him when we pray. We talk when we are lonely, sad, happy, worried or any other time. Enjoy your prayers to God. He will always listen and understand the prayers of the righteous. When I talk with couples who are having problems, many times I hear either one or both say, "You don't listen to me!" **God always listens to his children!**

<u>We rejoice when God is with us during sickness! We can know that God is there with us.</u> Jesus healed many people while he was on the earth. His actions show how concerned God is with the sick. We need the medicines which are for diseases, and we need the doctors and nurses who know which medicines to give us. A doctor told me, "I can perform the surgery you need. Only God can heal your body." The surgeon did his work well, and God healed my body.

<u>We rejoice that God is with us in death!</u> While Christians live on the earth, they are in God's care. **When we die, we are still in his care.** He doesn't forget about us because we are no longer on the earth. I don't know much about after death. We enter a spirit world which human eyes cannot see. God can see in that world as well as in this physical world.

Rejoice in the Lord always!
Love, Vernon   *01-16-11*

Ladders ~

There is much said about the ladder of success in the business world. Are you moving up the ladder? Are you being kind to the fellow workers on your way to the top?

There is no ladder in the church. We don't move up in the church. There is not any promotion after you become a Christian. To be a Christian is to be a child of God. There are no important or unimportant Christians.

A Christian is a new creation! *"Therefore, if anyone is in Christ, he is a new creation; old things have passed away; behold, all things have become new"* (**2 Corinthians 5:16-17**). All people are created in the image of God (**Genesis 1:26**). Each Christian is made pure and sinless as Jesus. In that respect we are created like God, spiritually. So we are a new creation.

Christians are different from their former lives. *"For we have spent enough of our past lifetime in doing the will of the Gentiles-- when we walked in lewdness, lusts, drunkenness, revelries, drinking parties, and abominable idolatries. In regard to these, they think it strange that you do not run with them in the same flood of dissipation, speaking evil of you"* (**1 Peter 4:3-4**). I remember a man who became a Christian. He had been one who would drink and get into fights. When he tried to convert his drinking friends, they thought he was strange. They said he used to be a lot of fun. Now, all he wanted to do was talk about God. He was a new creation! He was made in the image of Christ.

We also must realize that a Christian is one who is forgiven of sins. When we are forgiven we cannot become more forgiven. We as Christians can grow in grace and knowledge of our Lord and Savior Jesus Christ. You are expected to learn more and become stronger in your following of the Lord and avoiding sin. I do not wish to leave the impression that a new Christian is a full-grown Christian. *"For though by this time you ought to be teachers, you need someone to teach you again the first principles of the oracles of God; and you have come to need milk and not solid food. For everyone who partakes only of milk is unskilled in the word of righteousness, for he is a babe. But solid food belongs to those who are of full age, that is, those who by reason of use have their senses exercised to discern both good and evil"* (**Hebrews 5:12-14**).

Notice in the last part of the passage above, the Christian's senses are exercised. *You are to grow. Your growth must show others that you are maturing in the Lord.* We learn how to be like Christ by practicing Christianity.

One aspect of Christianity is not yielding to the temptations which are put before us. We are told, *"Therefore put to death your members which are on the earth: fornication, uncleanness, passion, evil desire, and covetousness, which is idolatry"* (**Colossians 3:5**). Many people are very diligent to avoid yielding to these sins.

Another aspect of Christianity is obeying the positive commands. *"Therefore, to him who knows to do good and does not do it, to him it is sin"* (**James 4:17**). Just as we are told not to steal – we are told to work! This is a good example of the negative and the positive.

The Lord has commanded us to go into **ALL** the world and preach the gospel to every creature. We are commanded to contend earnestly for the faith. We are commanded to pray. We are commanded to speak the truth in love. We are to worship God in spirit and truth. We must not forsake the assembling of the saints together. We must give as we have prospered. We must partake of the Lord's Supper. We must read and study the Bible. We must sing praises to God.

Love, Vernon
01-23-11

Mountain Experience ~

Mountain climbers are intrigued by the challenge of reaching the summit. The Christian is like a mountain climber because he wants to be closer to God. We believe that God is in heaven and therefore it is important that we become closer to him.

Moses had experiences on mountains. The first experience he had was on mount Horeb (**Exodus 3:1-12**). As he was herding his father-in-law's sheep, he saw a burning bush. He turned aside to see why it was not consumed. He had never seen anything like this before. When he came near the bush, God said to him, take your shoes off for you are standing on holy ground. He had been in this area for 40 years. God intended to send him back to Egypt. Moses was to lead the children of Israel out of the land of Egypt where they were slaves.

After he had led the children of Israel out of Egypt, Moses was instructed to go on to the top of Mount Sinai. There God gave him the Ten Commandments, the basis for the Law of Moses as we have it recorded in the Old Testament. While Moses was on Mount Sinai receiving the Ten Commandments, the children of Israel built a golden calf. When Moses saw their idol worship, he got so angry at them that he threw down the tablets of stones that the Ten Commandments were written on and broke them. When God decided to destroy the Israelites and to raise up a nation from Moses, Moses interceded for them and asked God to be merciful to them.

Moses also had an experience on the top of mount Nebo. His experience here was to look into the land of Canaan and view the beauties of it. As he was there on the mountain, he died and the angels buried him. He was not permitted to go into the land of

Canaan because he had disobeyed God. Moses was not lost eternally, but was punished because of his sins.

When Jesus was living on the earth, he took Peter, James, and John upon the mountaintop. There appeared at that time Elijah and Moses. They talked with Jesus concerning his coming death. Peter, not knowing what he should say, suggested that they build three tabernacles on the mountain; one for Jesus, Moses and Elijah. But God wanted us to know the importance of Jesus. So he said, *"this is my beloved son in whom I am pleased, hear you him"* (**Matthew 17:5**).

Today, we do not need to be on a mountaintop to worship God. The experience that we have in worshiping God is determined by the state of our hearts. If we worship God according to truth, then he is well pleased with us. If we worship God according to truth, then we will feel good about our worship because we have pleased God.

Abraham also worshiped on the mountain when he offered Isaac as a sacrifice to God. He did not actually kill Isaac, but as he drew the knife back to kill Isaac, God stopped him. God then knew that Abraham would do anything that he commanded him to do.

We also must be willing to obey God to any extent. He has not commanded us to kill someone. But he has commanded us to kill our sinful desires and to live our lives to the fullest extent in obedience unto righteousness. When our hearts are right with God, we will worship him in *"spirit and in truth"* (**John 4:24**).

Love, Vernon
01-30-11

Some Things Never Change ~

Do you remember in **Hebrews 13:8** it says, *"Jesus Christ the same yesterday today and forever."* There are many truths recorded in the Bible which never change. It is interesting that God is the same every day of every year all of our lives and throughout eternity. So we see that the truth in God's word will never change.

When God created man, He gave him the command to tend the garden of Eden. After Adam and Eve were driven from the garden, God continued with that command to work. Even in New Testament times God has commanded man to work: *"That you also aspire to lead a quiet life, to mind your own business, and to work with your own hands, as we commanded you, that you may walk properly toward those who are outside, and that you may lack nothing"* (**1 Thessalonians 4:11-12**). God never intended for man to be idle. You have heard people say that an idle mind is the devil's workshop. I don't think that is a quote from the Bible. It is certainly a *truth* from the Bible.

Another truth that will never change is the influence of evil people who influence others to be evil also. *"He who walks with wise men will be wise, but the companion of fools will be destroyed"* (**Proverbs 13:20**). This particular verse was written by Solomon about 1,000 years before Jesus came. There is another verse in the New Testament which Paul wrote after Jesus' ascension into heaven. *"Do not be deceived: evil company corrupts good habits"* (**1 Corinthians 15:33**). The reason that Paul could write this similar to what Solomon did was because this truth never changes.

Some people would try to tell us that the God of the Old Testament was not a God of love but a God of vengeance. But we see many times that God forgave his people for their sins because he is a God of love. He is a God of love even today. In **John chapter three, verse sixteen**, Jesus says that, *"God so loved the world that he gave his only begotten Son, that whoever believes in him should not perish but have everlasting life."* That God loved the people from the beginning of time cannot be questioned. This is a truth that will never change. The reason it will never change is recorded in **I John 4:8,** and states simply that, *"God is love."*

Another truth which is never changing is that God does not like sin. **Isaiah 59: 1-2** says that sin has separated them from God. Sin will separate us or anyone from God as long as the world stands. Sin is described in the Bible as darkness. God is described in the Bible as light. Light and darkness cannot exist together. When there is one, the other must be absent. Therefore when there is sin in the life of anyone, God cannot be in that same life. Just as sin separated the people from God during the time of Isaiah, so sin separates people from God even today.

God has always required obedience from his people. During the Old Testament times God gave some commands and some promises that would accompany those commands. God also gave some punishments that would accompany the disobedience of his commands. The commands that God has given for people to become Christians are commands which are recorded in the New Testament but were unheard of in the Old Testament. But the same commands that made people Christians in the first century are the same commands that will make people Christians in the twenty-first century. Paul says in **Galatians 1** that there is not another gospel. Today Jesus is the Savior of the world as he has been for about 2,000 years. <u>**The commands given to the people were for them to believe in God, to repent of their sins, to confess Jesus as God's son, and to be buried with Jesus in baptism for the remission of sins. These commands must be obeyed today to receive salvation.**</u>

Love, Vernon   *02-06-11*

A Special Day ~

Many people have days which they remember such as birthdays, weddings, anniversaries, graduation days, or the anniversary of a loved one passing away. Some of the special days bring happiness some bring sadness. They are special days.

God commanded the Jewish people in the Old Testament to observe certain days – the Passover, the Sabbath, the Day of Atonement and others. God even gave the punishment to be given to the people who did not honor these days. God has changed his law and these days are not to be observed as religious days toward God by Christians. We are under the New Testament. Christ died on the cross and took the old commandments away. **Colossians 2:14-17** says *"having wiped out the handwriting of requirements that was against us, which was contrary to us. And He has taken it out of the way, having nailed it to the cross, having disarmed principalities and powers, He made a public spectacle of them, triumphing over them in it. So let no one judge you in food or in drink, or regarding a festival or a new moon or Sabbaths, which are a shadow of things to come, but the substance is of Christ."*

Just as God changed the observance of the Old Testament days, he also changed the Old Testament food laws (**Read Acts 10:9-16**).

When we study the New Testament, we learn that the first day of the week has become important. Jesus arose from the dead on the first day of the week (**Matthew 28:1**). His disciples were together in the upper room on the first day of the week and Jesus appeared to them. The next Sunday they were together again and Jesus appeared to them!

We have an example of the disciples meeting on the first day of the week and partaking of the Lord's Supper in **Acts 20:7:** *"Now on the first day of the week, when the disciples came together to break bread, Paul, ready to depart the next day, spoke to them and*

"Words of Encouragement & Exhortation – 2011"   Curry

continued his message until midnight." Paul commanded the Christians to give on the first day of the week. *"Now concerning the collection for the saints, as I have given orders to the churches of Galatia, so you must do also: On the first day of the week let each one of you lay something aside, storing up as he may prosper, that there be no collections when I come"* (**1 Corinthians 16:1-2**).

So we see by these two passages the first day of the week is when the Christians met. We also have the reference of John being in the Spirit on the Lord's Day in Revelation **1:9-10**: *"I, John, both your brother and companion in the tribulation and kingdom and patience of Jesus Christ, was on the island that is called Patmos for the word of God and for the testimony of Jesus Christ. I was in the Spirit on the Lord's Day, and I heard behind me a loud voice, as of a trumpet,"*

A study of the New Testament shows it is fine to sing, pray and teach or preach on any day of the week. **But, when we meet on Sunday we observe all five acts of worship – partaking of the Lord's Supper, giving, singing, praying and preaching/teaching.**

We may meet any day of the week to sing, pray or teach. So some congregations have decided to meet during the middle of the week. Many congregations meet on Wednesday night, but some on Tuesday, and others on Thursday. During these worship services it is a sin to partake of the Lord's Supper or to take a collection.

There are other days which are special. Today is the day of salvation -- so today is special (**2 Corinthians 6:2**). Today is special because the Lord made it (**Psalms 118:24**). The Day of Judgment will be special – the righteous and unrighteous will be separated!

Love, Vernon
02-13-11

What Use Is It?

There are some things which have very little value. There are books which are of no value except to promote evil. Some of these books are written only to excite the lust of the flesh. The world would be a better place if these were not written. Some books are written to tell people how to worship themselves. These teach self-indulgence, and selfish ambitions. Some books teach people how to take advantage of other people's misfortune. What use are books of this nature?

There are many books which teach false doctrine. I have Darwin's *"The Origin of the Species"*. What use is the book? The writing of this book caused many people to question the truthfulness of the Bible. Still many today are struggling with the idea of evolution.

There are many religious books which teach contrary to the Bible. Baptism is a Bible subject taught very plainly in the scriptures. Many books have been written which teach that baptism is not necessary for salvation. These verses are plain concerning baptism: ***Mark 16:16**, "He who believes and is baptized will be saved; but he who does not believe will be condemned." **Acts 22:16**, "And now why are you waiting? Arise and be baptized, and wash away your sins, calling on the name of the Lord."* Of what use are books which teach contrary to the Bible.

Novels and adventure stories are interesting to read. Many people read them as a means of escaping into a state of mind which is relaxing to them. I enjoy reading the descriptions of the scenery in Zane Grey's novels. I can spend a lot of time reading and enjoying his writing. When I am finished with a book, am I any better for having read it? What is the use of books which are written to entertain?

"Words of Encouragement & Exhortation – 2011"   Curry

A few years back I bought several books from an older preacher. I haven't read all of them, yet. They are on my shelves. When I read one, then I know what the author has written. I can determine the truth of the book by comparing it to the Bible. If I do not read the books, what is the use of having them?

The Bible says: *"Your word is a lamp to my feet and a light to my path"* (**Psalms 119:105**).

"All Scripture is given by inspiration of God, and is profitable for doctrine, for reproof, for correction, for instruction in righteousness" (**2 Timothy 3:16**).

"It is the Spirit who gives life; the flesh profits nothing. The words that I speak to you are spirit, and they are life" (**John 6:63**).

"Sanctify them by Your truth. Your word is truth" (**John 17:17**). *"And, that from childhood you have known the Holy Scriptures, which are able to make you wise for salvation through faith which is in Christ Jesus"* (**2 Timothy 3:15**).

"The law of the LORD is perfect, converting the soul; The testimony of the LORD is sure, making wise the simple" (**Psalms 19:7**).

We can know the Bible was written for very good reasons. Yet, many people will not read or obey what they do read. You may have many Bibles in your house. If you do not read them, what use is the Bible to YOU? The Bible is good in every way! <u>You can learn it and obey God to the salvation of your soul</u>. If you do not study and obey the Bible, the next verse should scare you.

"He who rejects Me, and does not receive My words, has that which judges him--the word that I have spoken will judge him in the last day" (**John 12:48**).

Love, Vernon
02-20-11

Favorite Songs ~

The two verses which come to mind about singing are: **Ephesians 5:19:** *"speaking to one another in psalms and hymns and spiritual songs, singing and making melody in your heart to the Lord"* and **Colossians 3:16**: *"Let the word of Christ dwell in you richly in all wisdom, teaching and admonishing one another in psalms and hymns and spiritual songs, singing with grace in your hearts to the Lord."*

I suppose a third verse would be thought of also: **1 Corinthians 14:15:** *"What is the conclusion then? I will pray with the spirit, and I will also pray with the understanding. I will sing with the spirit, and I will also sing with the understanding."*

We know these verses should guide us in our singing. Songs must be scriptural and plain in their teaching. We must understand what the songs mean as we sing them. We sing some songs which glorify the Lord. Other songs prompt us to respond to the teaching of the gospel. Some songs teach us of the hope of glory. Other songs teach us of God's care for us in the life.

Songs have figures of speech in them just as the Bible has figures of speech. Jesus said, *"Again, the kingdom of heaven is like a merchant seeking beautiful pearls, 46 who, when he had found one pearl of great price, went and sold all that he had and bought it"* (**Matthew 13:45-46**).

Consider these words written by J.H. Sammis:
When we walk with the Lord
In the light of his word
What a glory he sheds on our way
While we do his good will

"Words of Encouragement & Exhortation – 2011"   Curry

He abides with us still
And with all who will trust and obey
Trust and obey for there's no other way
To be happy in Jesus but to trust and obey
You may recognize these words as the first verse and chorus to **_Trust and Obey._**

The words to your favorite song have special meaning for you. We must keep singing. It is God's command. Many songs have a special place in my life. Each one has teaching for me and others.

There may be another verse which you may think of: **James 5:13:** *"Is anyone among you suffering? Let him pray. Is anyone cheerful? Let him sing psalms."*

God bless us in our singing in the assembly and in our private lives.

Love, Vernon
02-27-11

Discipline for Good ~

Parents are to disciple their children. It is for the good of the children. Discipline is not to take away something good. It is given to prepare that person for a good life. We know those who do not obey the law will be punished! **We discipline our children to respect the law – the law of the land and the law of God!** We do not wish our children to be put into prison or even put to death because they break the law! We certainly want our children to respect and obey the law of God. The punishment of hell is harsher than any punishment of men. *"Harsh discipline is for him who forsakes the way, and he who hates correction will die"* (**Proverbs 15:10**).

We know that Jesus is the Way (**John 14:6**). In the book of **Acts** *"the Way"* is used eight times to refer to the Church. We must not forsake *"the Way"* of God. Harsh discipline does await those who neglect the Way! God does discipline us for our good. Read all of **Hebrews 12:7-11**. Note **verses 9 and 10** from the New American Standard Version, *"Furthermore, we had earthly fathers to discipline us, and we respected them; shall we not much rather be subject to the Father of spirits, and live? For they disciplined us for a short time as seemed best to them, but He disciplines us for our good, that we may share His holiness."* He contrasts the discipline of our parents with the discipline from God. When we submit to the discipline of God, we profit very much.

We are to discipline ourselves. We know the will of God. We must submit to God's will! We are the ones who are responsible for our obedience. Paul said this about himself: *"And everyone who competes for the prize is temperate in all things. Now they do it to obtain a perishable crown, but we for an imperishable crown. Therefore I run thus: not with uncertainty. Thus I fight: not as one who beats the air. But I discipline my body and bring it into subjection, lest, when I have preached to others, I myself should become disqualified"* (**1 Corinthians 9:25-27**). Christians are working for the prize of eternal life! Those who do not discipline themselves will not receive the prize. The word of God can guide us, but we must submit to obey to receive the prize. Fellow Christians can correct, encourage and rebuke, but each one is responsible for his own salvation!

Some will discipline themselves when they are around other Christians, but will not when they are around sinners! We must discipline ourselves all the time. *"Only let your conduct be worthy of the gospel of Christ, so that whether I come and see you or am absent, I may hear of your affairs, that you stand fast in one spirit, with one mind striving together for the faith of the gospel"* (**Philippians 1:27**).

There is a way to live for the Lord, and sin cannot overtake us if we discipline ourselves by the word. *"No temptation has overtaken you except such as is common to man; but God is faithful, who will not allow you to be tempted beyond what you are able, but with the temptation will also make the way of escape, that you may be able to bear it"* (**1 Corinthians 10:13**).

Many people think discipline by parents is spanking only. Discipline for children is teaching and showing and encouraging and yes, spanking! Many people think discipline in the church is disfellowshiping only. It includes teaching, encouraging, rebuking and yes, disfellowshiping. All discipline must be done in love, because we do love. We wish for all to live faithful to God. You must discipline yourself. *"Therefore, my beloved, as you have always obeyed, not as in my presence only, but now much more in my absence, work out your own salvation with fear and trembling"* (**Philippians 2:12**).

Love, Vernon
03-06-11

A Convenient Time ~

Have you considered that most of what we do is done when we have a convenient time? There are some things which are scheduled for us by others such as our work schedule, or our spouse's requests to do certain things. You know how we put off doing some things until a convenient time.

When Paul, the Apostle, was talking with Felix, the governor, the Bible says: *"Now as he reasoned about righteousness, self-control, and the judgment to come, Felix was afraid and answered, 'Go away for now; when I have a convenient time I will call for you' "* (**Acts 24:25**). Felix was touch by the gospel on this occasion. We know that because he was afraid!

That day was the time when Felix should have become a Christian. Many times people are touched by the gospel of Christ, but they put off obedience to that gospel. You may be one of those! **Please do not wait until a convenient time. You should obey when you learn the truth of the gospel.**

We have more information about Felix. He called for Paul often and listened to him hoping that Paul would offer him money for his release. So even though he heard the teaching of the gospel – he did not obey. The Bible never reveals if he found a convenient time!

If you are a Christian and a faithful worshiper of God, is there something you are waiting for a convenient time to do? Possibly, you have been waiting for a convenient time to teach someone the gospel. You may be waiting until…to visit a sick friend. You may be waiting…to take a lead in the worship services. You may be waiting…to begin teaching Bible classes. **Why do you wait? Today, is the time to change your life and get on the right way to obey God. It is as convenient today as it will be tomorrow.**

Was it a convenient day for Jesus to die on the cross? Certainly that was not the only place one could be on that day. Jesus was

"Words of Encouragement & Exhortation – 2011"   Curry

obeying God in his life! It is always the day to obey God. Jesus loved you so much that he chose that day to do God's will.

We have forgotten the urgency of obeying God. People have a tendency to believe they have more time. You know, by hearing or reading the news, that death comes to people of any age. We must let people know that today is the day of salvation. **Tomorrow may be too late. The convenient time is now!**

Sometimes we are upset when our sleep is disturbed. In **Mark chapter 4,** Jesus had taught the people all day. When evening came the disciples took the boats to go to the other side of the sea. Jesus went to sleep. A storm arose and the disciples came and woke Jesus. He stilled the storm. He did not complain because it was inconvenient for him.

We may complain when we must deal with problems because it is not a convenient time. In **Mark chapter 5**, Jesus is met by a man who had devils in him. Jesus cast them into the herd of swine and the man was whole! Later in the same chapter Jesus was going to Jarius' house to heal his daughter. A woman who desired to be healed came and touched the hem of his garment and was healed. Jesus asked who had touched him. He wasn't upset because it was inconvenient for him.

Children interrupt people and are scolded because it is not convenient. Years later the parents wonder why those children are not close to them – the parents now have time – maybe even lots of time. It is now not convenient for the children.

When you have the opportunity to do God's will or help a fellowman, do it then. Do not wait for a convenient time. It is always convenient to obey God. Do not put it off and be lost!

Love, Vernon
03-13-11

Ambitious for the Lord ~

Most of the time when we tell people to be ambitious, we are talking about earthly things. Have you considered that it is a good thing to be ambitious to please the Lord? In **2 Corinthians 5:9** (NASV), *"Therefore also we have as our ambition, whether at home or absent, to be pleasing to Him."*

So many people want a home in heaven, but they want to please themselves while living on the earth. We know how to please the Lord. He has told us in the Bible. **There are many people who say, "I can't live a Christian life." I ask you, which command from God can you not obey:**
1. To not forsake assembling with the saints.
2. Pray.
3. Sing.
4. Do good to all men.
5. Love your enemies.
6. Go and teach all nations.
7. Remember the Lord's death by partaking of the Lord's Supper
8. Have, so you will have to give to others.
9. Speak only good for edification.

This is certainly not a complete list of commands from God. How have you done so far? Are there any that you can't obey?

Let's look at a list of sins. You decide which one of these you cannot avoid: *"adultery, fornication, uncleanness, lewdness, idolatry, sorcery, hatred, contentions, jealousies, outbursts of wrath, selfish ambitions, dissensions, heresies, envy, murders, drunkenness, revelries, and the like"* (**Galatians 5:19-21**).

"Words of Encouragement & Exhortation – 2011"   Curry

One of the sins listed is selfish ambitions. Paul condemns that in other letters. *"Let nothing be done through selfish ambition or conceit, but in lowliness of mind let each esteem others better than himself"* (**Philippians 2:3**).

Ambition is neutral – neither right nor wrong. It all depends on the direction our ambition is taking us.

Love, Vernon
03-20-11

Productive Christians –

I recently heard someone use the term – counterproductive. Of course, that means not productive. Christians are to be productive. Christians must make wise use of their time and talents to be productive.

Jesus gave us the parable of the Sower in **Matthew 13:3-8,** and explains the parable in **verses 18-23**. We learn that some people who hear the word of God are not productive. Some do not produce because of unbelief, others because they yield to temptation. Each one who does produce does so at different rates. Some in the parable produced 30 times or 60 times or one hundred times.

In **Matthew 25:14-30**, Jesus gives us a parable concerning talents. Each person received a different number of talents. Each person produced a different number from what they were given. Notice as you read this passage the one who produced two talents received praise just as the one who produced five talents. This shows that each person is to use what they are given and not expect to be someone else! The man who was given one talent was condemned because he did not put it to use. He was afraid – so he was not productive! People who are afraid will be cast into hell **(Revelation 21:8)**. We all have ability to produce for the Lord! None of us are the same as others. We must not expect to produce the same as other Christians. We must all produce!

<u>**What are you to do?**</u> Do you see a void in the work of the congregation? Will you put forth the effort to fill that void? **Some work which may be needed:**
1. Bible class teachers for all ages.
2. Someone to preach occasionally.
3. Preachers for small congregations in this area.
4. Ushers during the worship services.
5. Someone to prepare communion.
6. Song leaders.

7. **Someone to visit the sick or shut-ins.**
8. **Someone to send cards of encouragement.**
9. **Someone to contact by card or phone those who miss worship.**

You may think of something else not in this short list. **Will you do the work which needs to be done?**

Christians can be trained to do the work of the Lord. That can be easily understood. All people need to be trained for the jobs they do – teachers, bus drivers, plumbers, railroad workers, etc. Some people go to college for four years to receive the needed training for their profession. Others may go to college for even twelve years to receive their training! The training these receive is necessary for their profession. Doing the work Christians do is even more important than any physical job. **We must be willing to be trained to do the work of a Christian.**

It is possible for a Christian to be self- trained. The book which we all must follow is the Bible. Any average person can study and learn the Bible. This isn't learned in just a few minutes or even days. It takes a life time and then we still are learning. A preacher was talking about helping his father prepare for a debate. His father was an old preacher and an experienced debater. To prepare for the debate the father studied all he could find written on the subject to be debated. He studied for several hours each day for six months. He wanted to be productive in the debate. His son had not debated and did not know the need for training for each debate in that *fashion.*

You will learn many things by reading books written by men about the Bible. We may be trained by others through their books or in the classroom; either way, we are receiving training.

The more trained a person is, the more productive one can be. In our training we must remember to pray to God for wisdom. We must have knowledge and know how to apply that knowledge in teaching or helping others. Prepare to be productive.

Love, Vernon   *03-27-11*

Enjoy the Trip ~

Many times people take a trip to visit a specific person or place. Some trips are traveled for an important event so arrival time is important. Other trips do not have a strict time to arrive so there may be side adventures...

Do you think of Christianity as a journey? We are on our way to heaven to live eternally with God. The end is worth all the heartache or trouble we have on the journey. Are you happy that you are a Christian? Are you enjoying the trip?

The most joyful occasion for me is when a person obeys the gospel. To see one baptized into Christ brings great pleasure for me. Some people might think it is like seeing the sunshine after a dreary day. I do not believe the only joyful occasion in my Christian life should be when someone is baptized. **So let's look at other pleasures of living as a Christian.**

Prayer is part of the trip – did you have pleasure in prayer today? Praying is a command which Christians obey every day, even several times daily. Is praying a pleasure – or a chore? Do you ever feel real happiness when praying? You are praying to the God of heaven. He loves you so much he has given Jesus to die for you. You are permitted to speak to him! He is the greatest being ever! He is always in his glory and grandeur! **He is the creator and sustainer of life! He will take time to hear your prayers!** Such great pleasure is given only to Christians! Christians just can't wait for a time when they can pray to God about it all! He will listen as we tell him our sadness. He will show his love to us because of the sadness! He will listen to us in our joy. He rejoices with us in our happiness!

Do you have pleasure in reading God's word today? Reading and studying God's word is a command Christians obey. Is it a pleasure or a chore for you to read the Bible? God is the one who knows everything! Not just about you, but he knows everything! He made the world which mankind is exploring. We try to find out how things are made and how they work. God knows he is the creator of these things which seem so complex to us. He knows what makes us act and say the things which we do! He knows exactly what we are to do to have a good relationship with him. God has even revealed to us this plan he has made. We can read it in the Bible! Have you felt the joy of hearing God's word in your mind today? It pleases God when you read his word. Does it please you? Are you enjoying the trip?

It pleases God when you visit the sick, sad, lonely, and down-trodden. God is pleased when you worship him with fellow Christians! God is pleased when you teach and admonish others.

Are you the person who only does what God commands because you believe it is a must to reach heaven? Are you obeying God because it makes you happy? We know God wants all to obey him. I am afraid that some obey only because they fear. It doesn't seem to bring them any pleasure! Do you want to go to heaven? Are you having pleasure on the trip?

Consider this verse: *"Now, Lord, look on their threats, and grant to your servants that with all boldness they may speak your word"* (**Acts 4:29**). Consider this verse: *"So they departed from the presence of the council, rejoicing that they were counted worthy to suffer shame for His name"* (**Acts 5:41**). Consider this verse: *"I say to you that likewise there will be more joy in heaven over one sinner who repents than over ninety-nine just persons who need no repentance"* (**Luke 15:7**).

I really believe we need to work on enjoying the journey through this life on the way to a better country!

Love, Vernon
04-03-11

Silence ~

"Silence is golden." I do not know the first person to say that. It sounds like a quote from one who hears a lot of words! There is a time to remain silent. The idols of men cannot speak. The God of heaven can speak (**Habakkuk 2:20**). We must be ready to hear his words. God spoke through prophets during the Old Testament. He has spoken to us through his son (**Hebrews 1:1-2**). The words which he has given to us are very important. They are spirit and life (**John 6:63**). It would be disastrous for men if God was silent. *"Do not keep silent, O God!"* (**Psalms 83:1**).

There are times when people should be silent: *"And where there is no talebearer, strife ceases"* (**Proverbs 26:20**). *"A perverse man sows strife, and a whisperer separates the best of friends"* (**Proverbs 16:28**). *"Cast out the scoffer, and contention will leave; yes, strife and reproach will cease"* (**Proverbs 22:10**). *"The words of a talebearer are like tasty trifles, and they go down into the inmost body"* (**Proverbs 26:22**). *"And the tongue is a fire, a world of iniquity. The tongue is so set among our members that it defiles the whole body, and sets on fire the course of nature; and it is set on fire by hell"* (**James 3:6**).

We are to talk for good and not bad. Sometimes people tell the truth and it hurts individual Christians, even the Lord's church. Think about this passage *"Let no corrupt word proceed out of your mouth, but what is good for necessary edification, that it may impart grace to the hearers"* (**Ephesians 4:29**). Words which are not good for necessary edification are words which should not be spoken! Criticisms spoken about others (when they are not present) do not edify. **<u>Think before you talk</u>**. If your words should not be spoken, then silence is golden! Gold is worth a great price and so is silence. So there *can* certainly be times when your speech is sinful!

There is also times when silence is sinful. Consider a couple passages. *"But Peter and John answered and said to them, Whether it is right in the sight of God to listen to you more than to God, you judge. For we cannot but speak the things which we have seen and heard"* (**Acts 4:19-20**). The apostles knew they must speak the words of God! When we will not speak the words of God, we are sinning.

God has given the responsibility of speaking the gospel to the lost to Christians. Paul felt a necessity to preach. *"For if I preach the gospel, I have nothing to boast of, for necessity is laid upon me; yes, woe is me if I do not preach the gospel!"* (**1 Corinthians 9:16**). As with the apostles, we also must feel the necessity of preaching the gospel. Silence then becomes rotten instead of golden.

Some become discouraged in preaching. Jeremiah was one who did. *"Then I said, 'I will not make mention of Him, nor speak anymore in His name. But His word was in my heart like a burning fire, shut up in my bones"* (**Jeremiah 20:9**). We too may become discouraged. People will not listen when we teach the word! People refuse even to believe the word. They do not obey! Why should we continue to speak? Is it time for silence? Read again the last part of **Jeremiah 20:9**: *"But His word was in my heart like a burning fire, shut up in my bones;"*

We know the gospel is the power of God to salvation! We know God is not willing that any should perish! How can they hear without a preacher! Continue to speak the truth from God. The word of God will give them life!

<u>**May God grant us the wisdom to know when to speak and when to be silent.**</u>

Love, Vernon
04-10-11

Preach the Word ~

The Bible is from God. *"All Scripture is given by inspiration of God, and is profitable for doctrine, for reproof, for correction, for instruction in righteousness"* (**2 Timothy 3:16**). That is the reason for preaching the word. <u>Everything the church needs as far as the teaching and practice of Christianity is concerned is included in the Word.</u>

All "Christian" churches preach part of the word. Many have written in book form their doctrine. They have written their belief of how to become a Christian, and how to worship God. They have written what they believe about healing and the Holy Spirit. They have written on many other topics in their 'official' book! Any teaching or practice that is not **exactly what the Bible says** is not sufficient for the 'official' book of the church. There are many articles written about one or the other subjects (such as this one). These articles are not accepted as the 'official' stand of the church. **We must believe and practice the entire word of God. When we accept just a part of the Word we have not obeyed God.**

<u>**The preaching of the Word leads people to be Christians**</u>. *When anyone preaches only a part of the word, they are sinning. Preaching the official doctrine or creed of a denomination will not make a person a Christian. It will only make a person a member of that denomination whose doctrine is proclaimed.*

Some teach we are saved by grace only. This teaching says there is no response needed from man to become a Christian. **There is nowhere in the Bible that salvation by grace only is taught**. I encourage you to read the book of **Acts** and understand those people **DID** something to become Christians. *Faith is necessary for anyone to become a Christian.* *"But without faith it is impossible to please Him, for he who comes to God must believe that He is, and that He is a rewarder of those who diligently seek*

Him" (**Hebrews 11:6**). Again, some doctrines teach one is saved by faith only. They quote verses such as **Acts 16:30-31:** *"And he brought them out and said, "Sirs, what must I do to be saved?"* So they said, <u>*"Believe on the Lord Jesus Christ, and you will be saved, you and your household."*</u> The people then say there it is - faith only. Will you read a few more verses in the same place? **Acts 16:32-33:** *"Then they spoke the word of the Lord to him and to all who were in his house. And he took them the same hour of the night and washed their stripes. And immediately he and all his family were baptized."* The washing of their stripes shows a change of heart, 'repentance'. Baptism is for the remission of sins (**Acts 2:38 and Acts 22:16**). Remember Jesus taught, *"He who believes and is baptized will be saved; but he who does not believe will be condemned"* (**Mark 16:16**). To conclude the thought of salvation by faith only, faith only is used only once in the Bible: *"You see then that a man is justified by works, and not by faith only"* (**James 2:24**).

When the word is preached, it will save those who hear it and obey it. There is no place for teaching or believing only part of the word.

Consider this about the word. It is inspired by God. Jesus is spoken of as the Word of God. John 1:1-2: *"In the beginning was the Word, and the Word was with God, and the Word was God. He was in the beginning with God."* John 1:14: *"And the Word became flesh and dwelt among us, and we beheld His glory, the glory as of the only begotten of the Father, full of grace and truth."* **When anyone rejects a part of the Bible they are rejecting a part of the Son of God.** <u>Everything which God has given men to write in the Bible is important. Let's study it all and be obedient to God!</u>

May God bless each of us with the determination and wisdom to fully obey the Bible, his word!

Love, Vernon
04-17-11

How to Shake the Past!

Everyone has a past. Some people do not want to escape their past. They enjoy the precious memories of it. We can't get away from our past, even though we may not enjoy the memories of it. I have noticed that when I go somewhere to get away from myself, I am there too! So if you are one of those people who wants to forget their past – how do you shake it?

I have thought a lot about this. One thing that seems to be apparent is forgiveness. Some cannot forgive themselves of past sins. In fact, some cannot accept the forgiveness of past sins from God. Some people despise themselves so much they cannot believe that God can love them!

The people who crucified Jesus could be forgiven. Now that was a very serious sin. The people had been a part of the death of Jesus, the Son of God. Notice what they were told they must do to have remission/forgiveness of sins: **Acts 2:38**, *"Then Peter said to them,'Repent, and let every one of you be baptized in the name of Jesus Christ for the remission of sins; and you shall receive the gift of the Holy Spirit."* Have you committed a sin which is worse?

Saul of Tarsus, whom we know as Paul the apostle, was a sinful person. Read these passages carefully. The man described in them was forgiven! *"...and they cast him out of the city and stoned him. And the witnesses laid down their clothes at the feet of a young man named Saul. And they stoned Stephen as he was calling on God and saying, 'Lord Jesus, receive my spirit"* (**Acts 7:58-59**).

"Indeed, I myself thought I must do many things contrary to the name of Jesus of Nazareth. This I also did in Jerusalem, and many of the saints I shut up in prison, having received authority from the chief priests; and when they were put to death, I cast my vote

against them. And I punished them often in every synagogue and compelled them to blaspheme; and being exceedingly enraged against them, I persecuted them even to foreign cities" (**Acts 26:9-11**).

"For you have heard of my former conduct in Judaism, how I persecuted the church of God beyond measure and tried to destroy it" (**Galatians 1:13**).

"Although I was formerly a blasphemer, a persecutor, and an insolent man; but I obtained mercy because I did it ignorantly in unbelief" (**1 Timothy 1:13**).

In the last passage, Paul said, *I obtained mercy."* He obeyed the gospel just as the people did as recorded on **Acts chapter 2**. He was commanded to *"Arise and be baptized, and wash away your sins, calling on the name of the Lord"* (**Acts 22:16**).

So far, we have spoken of forgiveness which is from God. After Paul became a Christian, what did he think about? *"Brethren, I do not count myself to have apprehended; but one thing I do, forgetting those things which are behind and reaching forward to those things which are ahead, I press toward the goal for the prize of the upward call of God in Christ Jesus. Therefore let us, as many as are mature, have this mind; and if in anything you think otherwise, God will reveal even this to you"* (**Philippians 3:13-15**).

<u>Had Paul forgotten his past? NO! He had shaken it off and was looking toward the future! He remembered, but he had a life to live for God. He could not dwell on his past and be the productive Christian that God expected him to be.</u> You cannot live in the past and produce fruit for God today.

If God has forgiven you, are you greater than God that you can condemn yourself? You understand that God is the judge of others. He is the judge of YOU also. Do not try to take his place! Accept God's forgiveness. Put your faith in God and his promises.

Love, Vernon   *05-01-11*

How to Shake the Past –

Last week I wrote about accepting the fact that God has forgiven you when you obeyed the Gospel. I also mentioned that you must forgive yourself! Today, I want to write about you forgiving others.

We know that God will not forgive an unforgiving person. *"For if you forgive men their trespasses, your heavenly Father will also forgive you. But if you do not forgive men their trespasses, neither will your Father forgive your trespasses"* (**Matthew 6:14-15**). I have heard many good discussions about -- should we forgive a person who will not repent? I feel sometimes that people are looking for a reason not to forgive. But they surely aren't! Our forgiveness does not put that person in a right relationship with God. God must forgive them for that relationship to be mended. We know that God will forgive when a person repents and obeys the commands of God.

We must obey the commands of God when someone sins against us. There are two commands which we must observe in dealing with this subject. **The first command** is found in **Matthew 5:23-24**: *"Therefore if you bring your gift to the altar, and there remember that your brother has something against you, leave your gift there before the altar, and go your way. First be reconciled to your brother, and then come and offer your gift."* When you know that a brother has something against you, it is your responsibility to go to that brother. I don't know whose fault it is. This verse does not place blame. It just points out the break in fellowship should be repaired. You are responsible for the effort of reconciliation.

The second command is found in **Matthew 18:15**: *"Moreover if your brother sins against you, go and tell him his fault between you and him alone. If he hears you, you have gained your brother."*

"Words of Encouragement & Exhortation – 2011"   Curry

This sin comes from the other person. So you have something against them. You are to go to them. You are responsible for the effort of reconciliation. So it isn't as the world thinks. They think the one who has wronged them must make the first move. A Christian is always responsible to make the first move. So if you need to work through something with someone, it is your move (Refer to **Matthew 18:15-17**).

May I add some advice about dealing with life? Many times the problems cannot be worked through as God would have us to do because one will not. Sometimes we have waited so long to work through the problem that the other person has died. In either of these situations, the solution is out of our hands. The advice I wish to give is about our heart.

Whether we forgive someone is important. Our relationship with them may not be mended if they are not willing. We must deal with the problem in the best way possible for our life. We must keep a tender heart. *"And be kind to one another, tenderhearted, forgiving one another, just as God in Christ forgave you"* (**Ephesians 4:32**). Our salvation (relationship with God) depends on how we feel toward others.

It is really sad when people go through life having resentment toward someone. Many times they will not tell the person. They will tell others, but never deal with the problem they have in their heart.

One closing thought. **We may need to forgive someone more than one time.** Peter realized this as he asked Jesus how many times he should forgive his bother. *"Then Peter came to Him and said, "Lord, how often shall my brother sin against me, and I forgive him? Up to seven times?"* Jesus said to him, *"I do not say to you, up to seven times, but up to seventy times seven"* (**Matthew 18:21-22**). *"Behold, how good and how pleasant it is for brethren to dwell together in unity!"* (**Psalms 133:1**).

Love, Vernon   *05-08-11*

You Shall Surely Die ~

The title is taken from **Genesis 2:17**. God made man and commanded among other things for them not to touch or eat of the tree of knowledge. You know they did eat of the fruit of the tree and they were driven from the garden. They died years later because of that sin. We die because of the sin which Adam committed (**Romans 5:12**). So it is true of each person living, *"You shall surely die."*

I remember years ago when I was 33 years of age. A fellow Christian had terminal cancer. I asked him how he was doing. He said, "I feel fine, but I know I am dying." Then He said, "You are too, but you haven't admitted it yet." Then when I was 37 years of age, a man in our community was found dead. The report was his death was from natural causes. I did not tell anyone at the time, but I knew then I *'might'* die. It is so hard for me and maybe you to admit that we are dying. I am now in my sixties. I still am not sure that my mind has accepted the fact that I am dying. Oh, as far as I know, I'm not sick. But then we must remember *'you shall surely die'*.

When Adam and Eve ate of the forbidden fruit, they died spiritually! We are told in **Isaiah 59:1, 2** that sin separates us from God. So they were separated from God by their sin. The reason they hid from God (**Genesis 3:8**) was because they had sinned against God.

When a person is of the age to be accountable to God for their actions, and they sin, they die spiritually. They are separated from God. Anyone separated from God is in a lost state. **God does not want any to be lost (2 Peter 3:9).** God certainly isn't going to become sinful so sinners will not be separated from him. God knew man needed a way to be reconciled to him: *"That is, that God was* *in Christ reconciling the world to Himself, not imputing their trespasses to them, and has committed to us the word of reconciliation. Now then, we are ambassadors for Christ, as though God were pleading through us: we implore you on Christ's behalf, be reconciled to God. For He made Him who knew no sin to be sin for us, that we might become the righteousness of God in Him"* (**2 Corinthians 5:19-21**). God has blessed us so greatly in loving us enough to provide a way for us to have reconciliation to him.

All sinners must be reconciled to God through Jesus. Everyone has the same command to obey to receive reconciliation. Some people look upon the commands as restriction on reconciliation; it is not a restriction, but a plan God made. **Remember sin separates a person from God. God has determined the requirements for Him to receive a sinner back to him**. The death of Jesus is the sacrifice which made it possible for God to deliver the plan to us. Please obey His plan!

God's plan is for you to:

Hear His word (**Romans 10:17**),

Believe His word (**Hebrews 11:6,**)

Repent of your sins (Acts 17:30),

Confess Jesus as God's Son (**Acts 8:37**),

And Be *baptized* for remission of sins (**Acts 2:38**)

You separate yourself from God by sinning. He reconciles (takes away your sins) you to himself by His **plan**. So a person becomes a sinner by themselves. **God makes a sinner righteous because they have obeyed His plan.**

If you are not a Christian, then you need to become one by obeying God's plan. A Christian is a new creature in Christ. The old man is dead; the new man is alive in Christ (**Romans 6:4; Galatians 2:20**).

Those whom God has reconciled to himself by his plan will never die (**John 11:26; Revelation 20:6**). When a Christian dies the physical death, they are not separated from God!

Love, Vernon   *05-15-11*

My Want List --

Dear Santa Claus, please check your good list and find my name on it. I want a little red wagon, a new game for my computer, a new TV and lots of other toys.

Our Father in heaven, please look down upon us with tender mercy. I want my Granny to get well. I want the sun to shine**. I want, I want, I want…**

Santa is just a made-up individual. God is real! We sometimes approach them alike. As a child we asked Santa once a year. As adults, so many people ask God only as a last resort.

It is right to pray for good health, sun, rain, wisdom and many more things which God does give to us.

We need a thank-you list also! We must learn to be thankful to God for all the good things which he gives. I sometimes read in *Dear Annie* that some person did not receive a thank you for gifts given. They wonder if they should quit sending gifts. If God quit sending you gifts because you did not say thank you, what would your life be like?

All of our prayers must be 'if it is God's will.' We never should want anything except what God wants!

Confrontation –

I do not like disagreements. So I choose to talk with people who will agree with me. That isn't the way we should think. **Sinners must be confronted with their sins. The religious person who is in sin must be confronted with the truth**. You know this will bring disagreements. Confronting is the way of Christ. He confronted the Pharisees and others who were wrong. John the Baptist confronted Herod who was living in sin.

When we confront, and we must confront, we must do so by speaking the truth in love. Love was the motivation for Jesus dying on the cross for your sins (**John 3:16**). Jesus did not come to condemn the world. He came to save the world. When our teaching is done only to condemn the world, it has the wrong motivation. Our teaching must be done to save the world!

Live Like Jesus –

There is a song which has the thought of following Jesus. It goes something like: "Are you walking in His footsteps; are you always doing good?" Jesus did no sin. He has set a high standard for our lives. Jesus went about doing good. He set a high standard for our lives.

We know by the Bible how Jesus lived and how he taught. We can know how he wants us to think, talk and act! We need to pursue the knowledge of Jesus and pattern our lives according to that knowledge.

The fruit of the spirit is: *"love, joy, peace, longsuffering, kindness, goodness, faithfulness, gentleness, self-control"* (**Galatians 5:22-23**). Here is a list of attributes we are to develop in our lives. This isn't a long or difficult list.

We are given a list of things we are to add to our lives in **2 Peter 1:5-7**, *"add to your faith virtue, to virtue knowledge, to knowledge self-control, to self-control perseverance, to perseverance godliness, to godliness brotherly kindness, and to brotherly kindness love."* This also is an easy list.

"A new commandment I give to you, that you love one another; as I have loved you, that you also love one another" (**John 13:34**).

"Take My yoke upon you and learn from Me, for I am gentle and lowly in heart, and you will find rest for your souls. For My yoke is easy and My burden is light" (**Matt 11:29-30**).

Love, Vernon   *05-22-11*

The Church ~

I am studying a book about the premillennial reign of Christ. One statement made by the author is the prophets did not prophesy about the church. I found that interesting! The author holds to the idea that Jesus came to establish His kingdom and the Jewish people would not accept him as king. Jesus then, according this writer, started the church.

Jesus had an opportunity to become an earthly king. *"Therefore when Jesus perceived that they were about to come and take Him by force to make Him king, He departed again to the mountain by Himself alone"* (**John 6:15**). To believe that God intended for Jesus to be an earthly king is contrary to this verse.

Think with me about the power of God. John, the Baptist, told the Jews *"For I say to you that God is able to raise up children to Abraham from these stones.* (**Matthew 3:9**). God took Gideon and three hundred men and defeated the enemy! God made the walls of Jericho fall. God raised Jesus from the dead. Jesus said in **Mark 10:27** all things are possible with God!

The kingdom of Jesus is not of this world (**John 18:36**). Did Jesus not know what he was talking about? Just before his death, Jesus said *"my hour has come!"* Did he think it was time for him to be made King? No. He knew it was time for him to die.

Let us notice some prophecies concerning the church. Peter quotes **Joel in Acts chapter 2**. He said the happenings on that day were a fulfillment of Joel's prophecy! Here in **Daniel** is a prophecy. *"And in the days of these kings the God of heaven will set up a kingdom which shall never be destroyed; and the kingdom shall not be left to other people; it shall break in pieces and consume all these kingdoms, and it shall stand forever"* (**Daniel 2:44**). Study the whole chapter. "**These kings**" mentioned in the first part of the verse are without question the kings of the Roman Empire. So God

"Words of Encouragement & Exhortation – 2011"   Curry

set up His kingdom during the reign of the Romans. **In Matthew 2**, John, the baptist, preached *"repent for the kingdom of heaven is at hand."* Then he gives a prophecy to prove he is telling the truth. He gives **Isaiah 40:3-4**. John was guided by the Holy Spirit and was not mistaken! **Isaiah 9:6-7** teaches us that Jesus will reign as king. **James** quotes from **Isaiah in Acts 15:16-17**, saying the prophecies were fulfilled in the first century.

That the kingdom existed during the first century is witnessed by the New Testament. Peter was given the keys to the kingdom and whatever was bound on earth would be bound in heaven! Peter is the one who spoke the first sermon telling Jews how to become Christians (**Acts 2:36-38**). Peter spoke the first sermon to Gentiles telling them how to become Christians (**Acts 10; 15:14**). Peter opened the door to the kingdom and invited the people to come in!

Paul in **Colossians 1:13** said *"He has delivered us from the power of darkness and conveyed us into the kingdom of the Son of His love."* Those people were in the kingdom. According to **Colossians 4:16,** Paul considered these people to also be members of the church. John, in **Revelation 1:9** says *"I, John, both your brother and companion in the tribulation and kingdom and patience of Jesus Christ,"* We have no doubt that John understood himself, as well as the seven churches of Asia, to be in the kingdom.

In conclusion, we know the kingdom which God promised to establish through the prophets is indeed the church of which we are members today. God did not fail in the first century to make Jesus king. He is the king of the kingdom of God. <u>**Jesus is the head of the church which is his body. Those who obey the gospel (the saved) are added to the church by the Lord.**</u>

Love, Vernon
05-29-11

The End is Near!

"But the prophet who presumes to speak a word in My name, which I have not commanded him to speak, or who speaks in the name of other gods, that prophet shall die.' "And if you say in your heart, 'How shall we know the word which the LORD has not spoken?'-- when a prophet speaks in the name of the LORD, if the thing does not happen or come to pass, that is the thing which the LORD has not spoken; the prophet has spoken it presumptuously; you shall not be afraid of him" (**Deuteronomy 18:20-22**).

As you have read this passage, you know you should not be afraid of the man who prophesied the coming of Jesus on May 21. He now has stretched this until October 21. He is a false prophet and does not speak the words of God.

Notice what God has revealed about the second coming of Jesus. *"But concerning the times and the seasons, brethren, you have no need that I should write to you. For you yourselves know perfectly that the day of the Lord so comes as a thief in the night"* (**1 Thessalonians 5:1-2**).

"But the day of the Lord will come as a thief in the night, in which the heavens will pass away with a great noise, and the elements will melt with fervent heat; both the earth and the works that are in it will be burned up. Therefore, since all these things will be dissolved, what manner of persons ought you to be in holy conduct and godliness" (**2 Peter 3:10-11**).

"Remember therefore how you have received and heard; hold fast and repent. Therefore if you will not watch, I will come upon you as a thief, and you will not know what hour I will come upon you" (**Revelation 3:3**).

"Behold, I am coming as a thief. Blessed is he who watches, and keeps his garments, lest he walk naked and they see his shame" (**Revelation 16:15**).

All of these people who claim the signs of the end of the world are close are just as the man mentioned in the beginning of the article. They are false prophets. Many times a thief will break into houses or businesses and steal things. We all know this happens, but most are not prepared for it to happen at their own places.

A man who had lost a lot of things to thieves told me I should be putting locks on buildings. I told him I was going to. He nodded his head and said yes, but it will be after they have stolen what you have now. He may very well be right.

Jesus is coming. The earth will burn up. The things on the earth will be destroyed. All people from the beginning until the end will be judged by God. The righteous will be taken to heaven. The unrighteous will be condemned to hell. The abodes are forever. **There is no escape from hell**! No one will have the desire to leave heaven!

All these events could happen at any time. We need not be concerned about when! We just need to be ready everyday. We must *"Watch and pray."* The Lord is coming! How will you feel when he does come? *"Finally, there is laid up for me the crown of righteousness, which the Lord, the righteous Judge, will give to me on that Day, and not to me only but also to all who have loved His appearing"* (*2 Timothy 4:8*).

We sing the words, "Trust and obey, for there is no other way to be happy in Jesus, but to trust and obey!" We can be happy in Jesus here. When we trust and obey, we will be happy in eternity too!

The Lord hasn't given us the responsibility of determining when Jesus will return. He has given us the duty of obeying him. *"Therefore you also be ready, for the Son of Man is coming at an hour you do not expect"* (**Matthew 24:44**).

Love, Vernon
06-05-11

The Pressures of Life ~

The pressures of life are real. Everyone struggles. We must not look toward others and think they do not struggle. When I was young, I borrowed some money. I told an older friend I would be happy when I did not need to borrow money. I am sure he was amused. He had a good job, some rental property, both houses and farm land. He told me he wished he did not need to borrow money also. That year he borrowed money to pay his property taxes. I was struggling and he was also.

We must provide for our own Paul told Timothy, *"But if anyone does not provide for his own, and especially for those of his household, he has denied the faith and is worse than an unbeliever"* (**1 Timothy 5:8**). It isn't always a simple task to provide for our own! We must work, plan and manage in order to obey this command. Yet, we must believe that God has not left us alone. He will provide for us. He sends the sun and rain. He has promised, *But seek first the kingdom of God and His righteousness, and all these things shall be added to you"* (**Matthew 6:33**). He has given us responsibility about the physical necessities, but he blesses us with necessities.

We must train our children in the way they should go! We are to teach – God said it very plainly to the Israelites, *"You shall teach them diligently to your children, and shall talk of them when you sit in your house, when you walk by the way, when you lie down, and when you rise up"* (**Deuteronomy 6:7**). God said he was confident in Abraham that he would teach his children the Lord's commandments. Timothy's grandmother and mother are examples of godly women who taught Timothy the truth. It is heart-wrenching when our family does not obey God. We must keep teaching the truth. We must continue to live right before God.

"Words of Encouragement & Exhortation – 2011"   Curry

We must accept responsibility for our obedience. Those who do not obey God will be lost. *"Not everyone who says to Me, 'Lord, Lord,' shall enter the kingdom of heaven, but he who does the will of My Father in heaven"* (**Matthew 7:21**). It follows that if we are responsible for our decision concerning salvation, then everyone else must make their own decision. **God tells us we are not responsible for other people's sins.** *"The soul who sins shall die. The son shall not bear the guilt of the father, nor the father bear the guilt of the son. The righteousness of the righteous shall be upon himself, and the wickedness of the wicked shall be upon himself"* (**Ezekiel 18:20**).

We may see a family come into the worship – happy, talking and laughing. They may be driving a nice automobile, dressed in nice clothes. Rest assured they are struggling with life. You are not alone in struggles. Everyone feels the pressures of life.

Everyone is tempted by the devil. The temptations you are struggling with are common to man. *"No temptation has overtaken you except such as is common to man"* (**1 Corinthians 10:13a**). We like to think at times that we are different. Do you remember the old song which said something like, "No one know the troubles I've seen".

God has not left us alone under the pressures of life's temptations to sin. *"God is faithful, who will not allow you to be tempted beyond what you are able, but with the temptation will also make the way of escape, that you may be able to bear it"* (1 Corinthians 10:13b). God has taken care of us. **The pressures are real, but God is there for us.** *"And we know that God causes all things to work together for good to those who love God, to those who are called according to His purpose"* (**Romans 8:28 NAS**).

We are all in life together with God. Be strong.

Love, Vernon
06-12-11

What to Look for in A Church ~

I heard a preacher say recently there are 650 major denominations in the USA. I believe the reason is that people are looking for a church which meets their needs. Many churches are studying the population around their area and deciding what people are seeking in a church. They are putting forth the effort then to meet those needs.

Part of the idea may be they are learning the idea of service to our fellowman. This concept is in the Bible. Jesus said he came not to be served, but to serve, and to give his life a ransom for many. So many have picked up on the idea that service is the important reason why a church exists. We must be of service to people. In **Acts 6:1-7**, the church gave service to the ones who needed food! This is a service. **Serving others is an important part of the work of the church**.

Notice what the twelve said in **Acts 6**, **verse 2**. *"It is not desirable that we should leave the word of God and serve tables."* The teaching of the word is what brings obedient faith to people. So we learn that teaching the word is important.

Salvation is very important. *"For what profit is it to a man if he gains the whole world, and loses his own soul? Or what will a man give in exchange for his soul?"* (**Matthew 16:26**). God knows the importance of food, but salvation is more important! Jesus knew what it was to be hungry. While he was hungry, Satan tempted him to turn some stones into bread. Jesus said, *"It is written, 'Man shall not live by bread alone, but by every word that proceeds from the mouth of God"* (Matthew 4:4).

Never let it be true that a Christian does not serve – even bread to the hungry. On the other hand, a Christian must never believe that physical food is more important than salvation. Physical food, emotional comfort, or fitting into the group is important – but salvation is much more important. Where salvation is, these other things will follow!

Let us think about the needs of the people in the area. They need to know that God loves them. God even loves the sinful person. He sends the rain on the just and the unjust. He sent Jesus his Son into the world so they could have salvation! God gives rain and sun so we may have the necessities of life. **He did not start the church so we would have the necessities of life. He started the church by Jesus' death which brings salvation from sin.**

Jesus came to seek and save the lost (**Luke 19:10**). This is what the people of the area need to know from the church. If the lost seek salvation, they must know what sin is! They must know how to be forgiven of sin. They must know how to worship and serve God.

A church is a group of called-out people. The church which Jesus built is the church of the saved. They are called from sin to righteousness (Acts 2:47). The Lord adds the saved to the church. Who of the community does not need salvation?

Some single people look for a church which has a singles' program. Some young families look for a church that has a youth program. Some older people look for a church that has an older adult program. Some churches are just groups of people who have programs for the various groups of people. They are fulfilling the needs of the people.

It isn't wrong to have programs for a group or groups of people. The church exists to bring the gospel to the people of the area. People are lost in sin. The church has the gospel. It is the power of God unto salvation! *People of the area are dying in sin seeking a church which meets their needs, but is not telling them the truth about sin and salvation!*

Look for a church which teaches and practices only the Bible. Salvation comes by obeying the gospel. Obey and be saved!

Love, Vernon   *06-19-11*

A Legend was in Our Town ~

I went to the Towers for lunch last Tuesday. I did not go just for lunch; I went to hear a legend fiddle player. Bea Hitt played the fiddle with a band. She has played music for most of her life. Her family has played music in this area for many years. She is only here for a few weeks visiting with her sister, Ruby Dunn.

I admire her faith and devotion to God, the Church of Christ, and the truth. She never plays music with religious songs. The band played at least one religious song. Sister Hitt sat down while they played that song. She has told some family members who play that Christians are to worship by singing not playing an instrument.

I want you to think of all the towns in Judea and Galilee that Jesus visited. He is a legend! Sister Hitt is just another Christian. **Jesus is the Only Begotten Son of God.** He traveled the area of the Jewish nation. He performed many miracles! He taught many lessons!

Do you remember the blind men by the road as Jesus came out of the city of Jericho? They asked him to heal their eyes. He did (**Matthew 20:29-34**)! Those men, their families and friends would talk about this man/legend for many years, possibly even generations! God had given the city of Jericho to Israel many years before. Joshua had led in the battle. God performed the miracle of the walls falling down! That legend is talked about even today, hundreds of years later! The miracle Jesus performed is just as great as that miracle! Yes, truly a legend came to town that day!

Please read **Mark 5:1-20**. Jesus came to the country of the Gadarenes. He met the man possessed of many demons. He cast these demons into a herd of swine. The man was sitting and listening to Jesus teach! How long do you think this miracle was spoken about? Many times Jesus would tell the people not to tell what he had done. This time he told the man to "go home to your

"Words of Encouragement & Exhortation – 2011"   Curry

friends and tell them"! This was the best thing to happen to this man. This man would tell the story over and over! Jesus is a legend in the area of Decapolis, where the man lived. Yes, truly a legend came to town that day!

Please read **Luke 7:11-17**. This was the day that Jesus visited the city of Nain. As Jesus entered the city, he met some who were having a funeral ceremony. A widow's only son had died. Jesus stopped the funeral and raised the man from the dead! *"And this report about Him went throughout all Judea and all the surrounding region"* (**Luke 7:17**). Would that mother ever forget what Jesus did? Jesus did this before a large crowd! There is no doubt of any of his miracles. He did not live in secret. Truly a legend came to Nain that day!

Please Read **John 6:60-69**. Jesus is teaching about life! **The words of Jesus changed the lives of people who knew him.** Some people became his followers. Some people hated Jesus because of his teaching. There was no one who heard him that remained the same as they were before! You also must make or may have already made a decision because of Jesus' words! When you heard his words, those words changed your life! I guess you could say a legend came to your town!

Are you a legend? Some people made history because of their inventions, writings, great deeds or their sacrifice for others. I think most of us are just ordinary people. When history books are written, our name will not be found in them! I think that in a few years, no one will remember us. When you think about Jesus and his power (the gospel), you realize we do not wish them to remember us. *We want others to remember the legend, Jesus the Son of God! This One has the words of eternal life! We must live by them in faithful obedience, and he will give us a home in heaven!*

Love, Vernon
06-26-11

60

You Can Do Mission Work ~

Jesus has not chosen the elite of this world to spread the gospel. Consider the apostles that Jesus chose. They were working people; four of them were fisherman and one a tax collector. Jesus sent them into all the world. Peter started out in Galilee. Tradition tells us that Peter ended his life in Rome. That is a long way from a fishing boat on the Sea of Galilee!

"And Jesus came and spoke to them, saying, 'All authority has been given to Me in heaven and on earth. <u>Go therefore and make disciples of all the nations,</u> baptizing them in the name of the Father and of the Son and of the Holy Spirit, teaching them to observe all things that I have commanded you; and lo, I am with you always, even to the end of the age. Amen" (**Matthew 28:18-20**).

Would you like to do mission work for Jesus? It may be a change for you to go to another country, but think about the change it was for Jesus to leave heaven and come to earth – for mission work! You may think you can't do mission work! Consider that mission work is not for you or me but for God.

Where should you go? There are all kinds of countries in the world. Some are very receptive, some are not very receptive, and then some are really hostile. How can you raise enough money to do mission work?
You may even wonder how much will it take!

You can go to the lost. There are many of them in every country. There are many lost in the United States! You are already here! **<u>The lost of our community need the gospel. You could be the one to make a difference in the lives of your neighbors</u>**. So the answer to the question, "Where should I go" is answered! I believe that all of us can afford to do mission work near our homes. So another question is answered, "How much money will it take?"

"Words of Encouragement & Exhortation – 2011"   Curry

How do you start the work? I have some suggestions:
1. *Pray for yourself that you may present the truth in love.*
2. *Pray for the person you plan to take the gospel to, that they will be receptive.*
3. *Decide what help you will use to teach the gospel such as a tract, Bible course, etc.*
4. *Ask a fellow Christian to go with you. Jesus sent his disciples in pairs.*
5. *Study the lesson so you know what you are going to teach.*
6. *If this is your first time, teach this lesson to your partner for practice.*
7. *You and your partner decide who is going to take the lead.*
8. *Pray that God will bless your mission work.*
9. Go and teach the gospel

You must never become discouraged. Jesus promised, *"I am with you always, even to the end of the age."* When we are living and working for Jesus, everything will be okay!

If you can go and talk, then you can do mission work. The gospel is the power of God to save. God has written the plan of salvation for you to use as you go into all the world! God is not willing that any should perish. You are his child and you must have the same goals that he has. He has given this gospel to you to take to the lost. Christians are the only missionaries that God has. If you do not go, someone is not taught!

Do you believe in Jesus? I know you do! Do you trust the gospel to change the lives of people? Do you trust God to be with you?

Do not delay your mission work anymore! The lost around you are depending on your coming to find them and teach them the gospel. It is true they may not know they are lost! You know! Will you tell them the gospel today?

Love, Vernon
07-03-11

You Can't Change the Past!

One reason the Lord said *'today is the day of salvation'* is that today is the only day we have. All the yesterdays which you have lived are gone. You have memories of some of the events of those years.

Let me give you an example of *'you can't change the past'*! While mowing my yard, the mower threw an object and broke a window in a car. I did not like having broken a window. There was not anything which I could do to undo the breakage! I just needed to replace the broken glass. I will remember the event. I will pay for the repair. I just can't change the past!

The Apostle Paul had memories of his past when he persecuted Christians. He could not change the past! During the time he persecuted Christians he was becoming an important person in the Jewish religion! He gave up that importance so he could be a Christian. *"Brethren, I do not count myself to have apprehended; but one thing I do, forgetting those things which are behind and reaching forward to those things which are ahead, I press toward the goal for the prize of the upward call of God in Christ Jesus"* **(Philippians 3:13-14)**. There is a difference in living in the past and having memories of it. It certainly isn't wrong to remember the past. There is no need to worry about the past because "you can't change the past"!

When we were living in sin, we thought on sinful things. Since becoming a Christian, we think on righteous things! God has given us some guidelines for thinking. *"Finally, brethren, whatever things are true, whatever things are noble, whatever things are just, whatever things are pure, whatever things are lovely, whatever things are of good report, if there is any virtue and if there is anything praiseworthy--meditate on these things"* **(Philippians 4:8)**. When our thoughts stay in these areas, then sinful desires will die.

"Words of Encouragement & Exhortation – 2011"   Curry

Jesus taught about not living in the past. *"No one, having put his hand to the plow, and looking back, is fit for the kingdom of God"* (**Luke 9:62**).

You may be ashamed of your past. You cannot change it. You may wish you had done things differently – you can't change it!

Okay, so you can't change the past -- now what?

When you became a Christian, you repented of your past sins. Your obedience to the Lord at baptism washed away your past sins. All things which you did sinful before have been forgiven by God! Christians who sin must repent and pray to God for forgiveness. When you obey that command, you are forgiven of your sins.

You may look back at your past and see all the sins. God looks at you as someone who is guiltless before him. He has taken away all your sins.

God desires you to live for him. Be like Jesus who went about doing good. Sinful people are living for themselves. You were when you were sinful. Now you are pure. So be holy as He who called you is holy! Being holy is not doing sinful things. It is also doing righteous deeds.

Start today to obey the Lord in everything at every time and in every way. You can't change the past, but you can sure live today so that when it is in the past, you will not want to change it!

You need to quit putting off doing right! *"Whatever your hand finds to do, do it with your might; for there is no work or device or knowledge or wisdom in the grave where you are going"* (**Ecclesiastic 9:10**). *"But by the grace of God I am what I am, and His grace toward me was not in vain; but I labored more abundantly than they all, yet not I, but the grace of God which was with me"* (1 **Corinthians 15:10**).

"Redeeming the time, because the days are evil" (**Ephesians 5:16**).

Love, Vernon   *07-10-11*

A Trip ~

We recently made a trip to Oklahoma for a family reunion. It was fun. Many people attended -- there were about 69 people there. While in the area, I attended Spiro Church of Christ in Spiro, Oklahoma. Sunday morning I listened as Wayne Curry presented a report about the India Mission Work. Sunday evening I presented the same report to Rena Road Church of Christ in Van Buren, Arkansas. These are two of several Churches of Christ who support our India Mission Work.

Wayne and Manly Gilpin have gone on into Oklahoma and Texas to report to four more churches that support us. In order for us to make the trip to India we must have the support of many churches. These churches will not continue to give if we quit reporting.

The trip to India is important so we can preach the gospel to the lost people there. The Christians there invite their friends and family to come and hear when we preach! I do not enjoy making that trip to India and back. I do enjoy the work while I am there.

There is another trip which is very important – the trip from this life into eternity! There are only two destinations for us in eternity – heaven or hell!

Hell is a place prepared for the devil and his angels. It is a place of darkness and torment. It is a place we want to avoid at all cost. This life may seem like a long time, but it is not. This life is short.

Heaven is a place prepared for Jesus and his disciples. When we call him Lord and do the things he has told us to do we are truly his disciples. It is a place of light, joy and love! Heaven holds only good. Hell holds only bad.

I have learned after many years to enjoy the trip, not just the time spent at the other end. We are to enjoy living a Christian life.

"Words of Encouragement & Exhortation – 2011"   Curry

Heaven will be great, but preparing for heaven should be a joyful occasion. So look at today! What can you find good about today?

Do you enjoy talking to God about your life? While at the family reunion I enjoyed visiting with everyone. While we are visiting fellow Christians we should enjoy those visits. How do you feel about attending worship and Bible classes? Those times are so very good. We sing to each other songs which praise God and edify each other. I know the voices of many people as I hear them singing! These fellow Christians are singing to me – of course everyone else is there also.

The public prayers which are said in the worship and classes are encouraging to me. I hear brothers praying for our nation, peace in the world, evangelism, the lost and the sick, plus many other things. I believe in God. He teaches us to pray! He is the one who hears those prayers! He answers those prayers! When I hear a prayer in public I know I am not alone in the world! Many other Christians are praying for similar things that I pray for in my private prayers! Praying is a happy time! We are talking to our heavenly Father!

We must read and meditate on God's word. When I read I know that God is speaking through those words of the Bible. I can know what he is like, how he wants me to be and how I am to treat other people. God has thought of everything we need to know to make the trip to heaven. He has told us how to enjoy the trip!

Love, Vernon
07-17-11

Teach the Gospel ~

There are many people who teach the gospel in its pure form. Listeners obey that doctrine and the Lord adds them to the church. You may have been influenced by a certain Christian or maybe many Christians. I attended Depoyster Church of Christ from 1949 until I was grown. The men who thought it good to build the church building there were: Brothers Turner, Norden and Brown. These men had their wives and other interested women alongside them in this effort. If this church building had not been built about the time I was born, what would I be? Many other Christians both men and women influenced me – and are still influencing me.

We may not influence a large number of people during our lifetime. We must put forth the effort to influence as many as possible. Today is the day for you to begin.

We must not always wait for someone to come to us for teaching. **We are commanded by Jesus to go and teach or preach the word.** *"Go therefore and make disciples of all the nations, baptizing them in the name of the Father and of the Son and of the Holy Spirit, teaching them to observe all things that I have commanded you; and lo, I am with you always, even to the end of the age. Amen"* (**Matthew 28:19-20**). *"And He said to them, 'Go into all the world and preach the gospel to every creature. He who believes and is baptized will be saved; but he who does not believe will be condemned"* (**16:15-16**).

The apostle Paul and his companions went many places preaching the word. There were teachers who stayed in Antioch and taught the word. *"Now in the church that was at Antioch there were certain prophets and teachers: Barnabas, Simeon who was called Niger, Lucius of Cyrene, Manaen who had been brought up* *with Herod the tetrarch, and Saul"* (**Acts 13:1-2**). We know from the next few verses that Barnabas and Saul (Paul) went on a mission trip. So that leaves Simeon who was called Niger, Lucius of Cyrene, and Manaen as teachers who stayed there and taught. The following chapters in **Acts** are about the travels of the missionaries. The ones who stayed in Antioch were just as important in the growth of the church. Following each trip Paul made he always came back to report of the success. The church in Antioch was strengthened both by the local teachers and the missionary reports.

In **Mark 16:15,** we are commanded to teach *'every creature'*. Today in your area there are people who are lost. We are the local Christians. **We are to do the teaching. Let us not wait for another to come and do mission work here!** Each generation must teach their families and friends. We must also teach the next generation.

There are many, many books which are written to help teach the gospel. Those may be helpful for you. The gospel is what you must teach. *"For I am not ashamed of the gospel of Christ, for <u>it is the power of God to salvation</u> for everyone who believes, for the Jew first and also for the Greek"* (**Romans 1:16**).

I have begun praying for a lady which I know that may be receptive to teach. Will you think of someone and begin praying for them. Pray for them every day this week. Pray also for yourself, that you will go and ask them to study with you. Pray for yourself so you will be able to say the right words in the right way. *"But, <u>speaking the truth in love</u>, may grow up in all things into Him who is the head—Christ"* (**Ephesians 4:15**).

When we plant the word, God will give the increase. When we do not teach, the sinners cannot obey! Love God enough to do his will.

Love, Vernon
07-24-11

Vacation Bible School

V ariety of Bible lessons
A ll are Welcome to come
C hrist is the leader to Heaven
A uthority was given to Jesus
T ruth will make you free
I nstruction is in the Bible
O ften people respond when taught
N eglect will bring destruction

B oys need Bible teaching
I ncreased knowledge of God
B abies are never too young to teach
L ove is from God
E nergy is in God's word

S tudents of all ages
C lasses so we learn more
H eaven is our goal
O pportunity for studying God's word
O pen learning to yourself
L iving for God

Please take advantage of this opportunity to learn more or to renew your knowledge of these special events in the Bible. Consider also the fellowship that you can have with fellow Christians.

Hear the Word of the Lord --

Americans listen to televisions, radios, all kinds of modern technologies. We listen to other people when they speak. Many have left out the most important person to listen to – the Lord!

The Jewish people had the opportunity to listen to the Lord. They did not know the scriptures, *"Jesus answered and said to them, 'You are mistaken, not knowing the Scriptures nor the power of God"* (**Matthew 22:29**). The group to whom Jesus is speaking is the Sadducees. They were attempting to trap Jesus by asking a question about marriage after the resurrection. The Sadducees people did not believe in the resurrection! They were mistaken in their teaching for two reasons: 1) not knowing the Scriptures 2) not knowing the power of God.

When we read the scriptures we can know the power of God! We can study the scriptures and learn what God has given for us to live by. **All scripture is from God**. The scripture is all we need for our spiritual life. *"All Scripture is given by inspiration of God, and is profitable for doctrine, for reproof, for correction, for instruction in righteousness, that the man of God may be complete, thoroughly equipped for every good work"* (**2 Timothy 3:16-17**).

We must study and be diligent to show ourselves approved by God to rightly divide the scriptures. *"Be diligent to present yourself approved to God, a worker who does not need to be ashamed, rightly dividing the word of truth"* (**2 Timothy 2:15**).

Give yourself over to a serious study of the word of the Lord. Hear him! Listen to his commands for you. Teach his word to others so they may obey the Lord.

Love, Vernon   *07-31-11*

Two Brothers --

There are many brothers mentioned in the Bible. There were Cain and Abel – Esau and Jacob - James and John – Andrew and Peter.

Cain and Abel were different. Cain was displeasing to God. Abel was pleasing to God. We know that Abel offered his sacrifice by faith. *"By faith Abel offered to God a more excellent sacrifice than Cain, through which he obtained witness that he was righteous, God testifying of his gifts; and through it he being dead still speaks"* (**Hebrews 11:4**). <u>God uses Abel and many others as examples in Hebrews 11 to teach us that faith is necessary to be pleasing to him.</u> We know that faith comes by hearing the word of God (**Romans 11:17**). It is impossible to please God if we do not hear his word. God has given us the Bible which is his word. We have the privilege to read or listen as others teach the Bible. Are you seeking to know God through his word? Will you worship and serve him by faith?

Esau and Jacob were different. Esau was a hairy person, while Jacob was smooth skinned. They were twins. Esau enjoyed hunting. There was a meat dish that he made which his father Isaac really enjoyed eating. He was to hunt meat and prepare the dish so his father would eat and bless him (Isaac was blind). Their mother knew of the plan so she encouraged Jacob to deceive Isaac. He killed a goat and Rebekah prepared the meat as Esau would prepare his. Jacob took it to his father pretending to be Esau. You may read this in **Genesis 25**. Esau became so angry he decided to kill Jacob. Rebekah knew of this so she asked Isaac to send Jacob away to her family to take himself a wife. Jacob stayed many years with his uncle. He married wives and accumulated many flocks and herds of animals. Time eventually came for him to return home. He was

"Words of Encouragement & Exhortation – 2011"   Curry

afraid of Esau even after all these years. When they finally meet, he learned that Esau had forgiven him and did not intend to kill him! Jacob still had guilty feelings after so many years. From these two brothers, we learn it is wrong to deceive! We learn it is good to reconcile so we may rid ourselves of guilt.

James and John lived during the time of Jesus. They were two of his apostles. They desired to be placed in positions of authority under Jesus. Jesus explained the greatest in the kingdom of heaven are the greatest servants. Many Christians have desired to be in authority in the church. They have desired it as the world does – power, not as Jesus – servant! As Jesus passed through one village, the people did not want to receive him. These brothers asked if they should call fire down from heaven and consume the village. Jesus rebuked them for this idea. They, like many Christians, learned that love is the way of God. God even loves his enemies (**Matthew 5:43-48**). We are taught in these same verses we are to love as God loves! James was killed in the early years of the church. John lived to be an old man.

Andrew and Peter were fishermen as were James and John. Andrew learned that Jesus was the Christ before Peter. He told his brother. There isn't much in the Bible about Andrew. Peter became a great spokesman for Christ. Andrew worked with small groups of people teaching them about Jesus. Peter on the other hand is recorded as preaching before many people. We know that each work is very important. When you read **Acts Chapter Two** where it says 3,000 people were baptized after the preaching – these were 3,000 individuals.

There are many brothers in the Bible. The closest are those who are Christians. Christians have different personalities; work at different occupations, etc. They are alike in that they have faith in the same God. These people are faithful to God through his word!

Love, Vernon   *08-07-11*

Walk with the Lord ~

I am amazed at the people who do not attend church anywhere, but they will pray and expect God to answer their prayers. Some people attend worship, but do not live according to the Lord and expect him to answer their prayers.

Living a Christian life is a walk with the Lord. Sinful people may try to hide from the Lord. Adam and Eve ate of the forbidden fruit then tried to hide from the Lord. *"And they heard the sound of the Lord God walking in the garden in the cool of the day, and Adam and his wife hid themselves from the presence of the LORD God among the trees of the garden"* (**Genesis 3:8**). It is implied they were accustomed to the Lord coming to the garden.

Sin has always separated mankind from God. This fact is stated in **Isaiah 59:1-2**: *"Behold, the Lord's hand is not shortened, that it cannot save; nor His ear heavy, that it cannot hear. but your iniquities have separated you from your God; and your sins have hidden His face from you, so that He will not hear."* Any time the Lord is not with someone, it isn't his fault! He never moves from people. People move from him. When we walk in the light, then we are walking with God! When we walk in sin/darkness, we are walking without God. He hasn't moved!

Walking with the Lord is more than avoiding sin. We must be going about doing good. Jesus did good. *"How God anointed Jesus of Nazareth with the Holy Spirit and with power, who went about doing good and healing all who were oppressed by the devil, for God was with Him"* (**Acts 10:38**). I have seen people who were always wanting others to do for them. They did not go about doing good! Now, whose side are they on? Certainly they are not like Jesus! We are taught *"And let us not grow weary while doing good,* *for in due season we shall reap if we do not lose heart. Therefore, as we have opportunity, let us do good to all, especially to those who are of the household of faith"* (**Galatians 6:9-10**). Some people would go to the other side of the street to keep from doing good. *"Then Jesus answered and said: "A certain man went down from Jerusalem to Jericho, and fell among thieves, who stripped him of his clothing, wounded him, and departed, leaving him half dead. Now by chance a certain priest came down that road. And when he saw him, he passed by on the other side. Likewise a Levite, when he arrived at the place, came and looked, and passed by on the other side"* (**Luke 10:30-32**).

The priests and Levites were to be the leaders of the people in religion. What about you? Are you a Christian? When is the last time you helped someone and was happy to do so?

You have heard the poem about the dash between the dates on the tomb stones. It represents the life of the person. The dates only represent the beginning and the end. In your dash can the Lord write – *"You went about doing good"*?

Those who walk with the Lord earnestly long for the appointed times to worship together. David said, *"I was glad when they said to me, "Let us go into the house of the LORD"* (**Psalms 122:1**). Some people come up with excuse after excuse for not worshiping. How do you feel about worship? When you walk with God, you will desire to be with fellow Christians. Some people use the excuse, "there are too many hypocrites in the Church," so they do not want to be around them. Hypocrites are going to hell. Those who choose not to worship are going to hell. It is better to be around them for a few years at worship than to spend eternity with them in hell.

Who are you walking with -- God or Satan? Who you walk with is the one you will spend eternity with.

Love, Vernon
08-14-11

The White of an Egg--

Job 6:6 Can flavorless food be eaten without salt? Or is there any taste in the white of an egg? People have always known what tastes good to them. I know some people cook the whites of eggs to eat for health reasons. I am not sure how they season them in that situation. The white has just about as little taste as anything I can think of.
Job 6:6 mentions putting salt on food. Life without God is flavorless. **Think of a few spiritual blessings which God gives Christians:**
   1. Forgiveness of sins – free from guilt
   2. Child status with God
   3. Christ as your brother
   4. Christ as your intercessor
   5. Holy Spirit as you intercessor
   6. Added to the church – family on earth
   7. Adoption by God
   9. Peace with God
   10. (You can add spiritual blessings which you think of.)

When Upon Life's Billows by Johnson Oatman
When upon life's billows you are tempest-tossed,
When you are discouraged thinking all is lost,
Count your many blessings; name them one by one,
And it will surprise you what the Lord has done.

Are you ever burdened with a load of care?
Does the cross seem heavy you are called to bear?
Count your many blessings, every doubt will fly.
And you will be singing as the days go by.
When you look at others with their land and gold,

Think that Christ has promised you His wealth untold.
Count your many blessings money cannot buy,
Your reward in heaven, nor your home on high.
So, amid the conflict, whether great or small,
Do not be discouraged, God is over all;
Count your many blessings,
Angels will attend, Help and comfort give you
   to your journey's end.

Count your many blessings; Name them one by one.
Count your many blessings; See what God hath done;
Count your many blessings, Name them one by one.
Count your many blessings, See what God hath done.

Christians are spoken of as the salt of the earth. *"You are the salt of the earth"* (**Matthew 5:13**). God has made a big difference in your life since you became a Christian. You are to make a difference in the lives of the people around you.

A small boy heard some adults talking many years ago. They said it was hot enough to fry an egg on the sidewalk. The boy tried that. He got an egg, broke it on the sidewalk, and immediately slurped it up. The white of that egg was not very good.

Life without God is tasteless. People lose all hope, all reason, and all spiritual blessings without God.

A Christian is made a new creature -- no cursing, no hating, no getting even, no remembering of wrongs done to them,

A Christian is made a new creature -- loving, forgiving, patient, happy, generous, etc.

Let God season your tasteless life! You will grow in favor with men and God.

Vernon Curry
8-21-11

In Order ~

Many people believe that God does not have an order to his commands today. They tend to stress the idea of believing only to have salvation. They express amazement at the idea that God has given a pattern.

I have heard people laugh at me when I have used examples from the Old Testament about being faithful to God's commands. There is the example of Nadab and Abihu being killed by God for offering fire which the Lord had not instructed them to use. I was asked, "Why use that? God isn't that way today."

God gave the children of Israel the order to lay the stones for the altar, the way to lay the meat, the fat and which fire to use. **God has given us the pattern to follow in the order which he has given it.**

To have salvation one must hear the word of God (**Romans 10:17**). *One must believe the word* (**Hebrews 11:6**). *One must repent of past sins and be converted* (**Acts 3:19**). *One must confess faith in Jesus as the Son of God* (**Acts 8:37**). *One must be baptized into Christ for the remission of sins* (**Galatians 3:27; Acts 2:38**). *One must call upon the name of the Lord* (**Acts 2:21**).

These are commands of God which must be obeyed. There is an order to them. When you put them in the wrong order, they just do not make any sense. For anyone to be baptized before hearing is impossible. How could one be baptized into Christ, if one has not heard of him? Why would one confess Jesus if faith is lacking? In **Acts 2:36-41**, all of the above commands are insinuated and obeyed by the ones who gladly received the word.

The worship of the church of Christ is to be decently and in order (**1 Corinthians 14:40**). Worship service which is confusion rather than orderly is not pleasing to God. When many people are talking at once, there is confusion. Read **1 Corinthians 14** and see the confusion they were having during their worship services. We are to do things in order so anyone can understand what is being done. *When some are praying and others singing at the same time, this isn't orderly.*

The orderliness of God is seen in the universe. The scientists are able to predict the exact location of the sun, moon or any of the stars at any particular time or day even years in advance. We know when spring starts because of the position of the sun. There is a false saying, *"before the end of time we can only tell the changing of the season by the budding of the trees."* People have attributed this saying to the Bible. Where they got that idea is beyond me! The end of the world will be just as any other day in the time of this earth.

The New Testament teaches about setting things in order. **Titus** is told he was left in Crete to set in order the things which were lacking. Then **Titus** is told the qualifications of elders and deacons. **There is order in the church of Christ because God has given the same commands to all the churches. The churches of Christ are made up of individuals who have obeyed from the heart the form/pattern or order which was given to them. This pattern is the same all over the world.**

Any group of people can call themselves the church of Christ. *They are the Church of Christ if they obey the commands of God.* If they do not obey the commands, they are not the Church of Christ – even if they call themselves by that name. Jesus prayed for unity among his followers in **John 17:20**. Unity can come only when obedience to God is by each person/congregation.

When our physical body is functioning in order, we have health. When parts of the body are not functioning orderly, we have sickness or death. The same is true of the Body of Christ – **the Church of Christ.**

Love, Vernon　　　　　*8-29-11*

"Words of Encouragement & Exhortation – 2011"   Curry

Labor Day --

The economy of the world is not good this year. Many people who are laborers in the workforce of the USA are unemployed. Therefore this holiday will not be a holiday for them. I encourage you to remember these unemployed people in your prayers. Most, if not all, of them wish they were employed. There have been times before when there were more workers than jobs. These times passed, as will this time. Hopefully better times are coming very soon.

When Jesus was here, he taught on the need for workers. *"Then He said to His disciples, 'The harvest truly is plentiful, but the laborers are few. Therefore pray the Lord of the harvest to send out laborers into His harvest"* (**Matthew 9:37-38**). The need hasn't changed at anytime during the past 2000 years, nor is it different today.

You need to be a worker today in the work of the Lord. Jesus doesn't have unemployment benefits. The reward is given to those who are workers. *"For the kingdom of heaven is like a landowner who went out early in the morning to hire laborers for his vineyard"* (**Matthew 20:1**). Read this chapter through verse 16. Notice he hired laborers for his vineyard. It did not matter what time they were hired. They were laborers. You must be about the business of the Lord.

The wicked and lazy servant in the parable of the talents was not pleasing to the Lord. His reward for doing nothing was: *"And cast the unprofitable servant into the outer darkness. There will be weeping and gnashing of teeth"* (**Matthew 25:30**). This one knew he was to work, but he was afraid!

Every day is Labor Day for the Christian. Christians don't retire, quit, or give up! How long has it been since you were working in the Lord's vineyard? We sing this song – and truly mean the words.

"Words of Encouragement & Exhortation – 2011"   Curry

I Want to be a Worker by I. Baltzell

I want to be a worker for the Lord; I want to love and trust His
   Holy word;
I want to sing and pray, and be busy every day,
In the vineyard of the Lord.

I want to be a worker every day; I want to lead the erring
   in the way
That leads to heav'n above, where all is peace and love,
In the kingdom of the Lord.

I want to be a worker strong and brave;
   I want to trust in Jesus' power to save;
All who will truly come, Shall find a happy home,
In the kingdom of the Lord.

I will work, I will pray, In the vineyard,
   in the vineyard of the Lord
I will work; I will pray,
   I will labor every day,
In the vineyard of the Lord.

   How long until the harvest is ripe. As you travel around our area you will see the corn and rice ripening. Open your eyes and look for the souls of men. These are ripe for the harvest. The time is now. Just as Jesus told the disciples. *"Do you not say, 'There are still four months and then comes the harvest? Behold, I say to you, lift up your eyes and look at the fields, for they are already white for harvest! And he who reaps receives wages, and gathers fruit for eternal life, that both he who sows and he who reaps may rejoice together"* (**John 4:35-36**).
   Christians who are not workers for the Lord will be disappointed on the Day of Judgment. Work today!

     Love, Vernon   ***09-04-11***

It's Not Anything!

While thinking of titles for articles, I thought of working for the Lord because last Monday was Labor Day. I thought September 11 this year was not anything. Then I checked the calendar. Today is Patriot Day. It is also Grandparents Day. Patriot Day is always September 11, while Grandparents Day is always the second Sunday in September.

Patriot Day is in memory of those who died on nine-eleven. There were three airplanes crashed that day killing 2,977 people. It is sad when anyone is murdered. The living are affected by this the rest of their lives. We do pray that the killing will stop in acts of terror, war, accidents and murders. Death brings sadness to the lives of the living.

Pray for our country and other countries of the world that peace may reign. We always pray the will of God be done. Patriots Day brings sad thoughts to my mind.

Today is also Grandparents Day! I don't know what grandparents are to do on this day – even though I am one! Maybe the grandchildren are to honor the grandparents. I don't know. The information I have found gives some light on the subject. The statute cites the day's purpose as: "...to honor grandparents, to give grandparents an opportunity to show love for their children's children, and to help children become aware of strength, information, and guidance older people can offer".

The Bible records that before the flood of Noah's time people lived to be several hundred years of age. Most of those people had many generations of ancestors living during their lifetime. Some today have five generations. There are some grandparents mentioned as examples of how people acted and thought.

Naomi lived to see her grandson, Obed. She was so happy when Boaz and Ruth had a son. She cared for that son!

"Then the women said to Naomi, "Blessed be the LORD, who has not left you this day without a close relative; and may his name be famous in Israel! 15 And may he be to you a restorer of life and a nourisher of your old age; for your daughter-in-law, who loves you, who is better to you than seven sons, has borne him." 16 Then Naomi took the child and laid him on her bosom, and became a nurse to him. 17 Also the neighbor women gave him a name, saying, "There is a son born to Naomi." And they called his name Obed. He is the father of Jesse, the father of David" **(Ruth 4:14-17).**

Other grandparents were Job and Lois. The greatest thing a grandparent can give to their grandchildren is the teaching of God. Many are able to leave possessions or money to them. These things perish with the using. The one who lives obedient to the Lord will have an everlasting home in heaven. God instructed Israel to teach their children and grandchildren the right way!

Spend time with your grandchildren. They will be better for the hours you are with them. You will be better for the hours they are with you. Be that old-fashioned person who believes in family get-togethers! Talk, laugh, cry and enjoy the youth of your family. Show them what love is. Show them respect -- don't just demand respect from them!

Care for them the way God cares for you. He is the Father in Heaven. He has provided us with a way to have forgiveness and a home in heaven with him. Pass this information on to your children and grandchildren and if you are blessed to live long enough to have great grandchildren, pass it on! God loves them!

Love, Vernon
09-11-11

It is Simple ~

Many people do not wish to become a Christian. A young man came once and asked, "How do we know there is a God?" This seemed like a good prospect to become a Christian. After a study of the scriptures, he understood there is a God. He said he believed this. He was told his next step was to repent of his sin and change the way he was living. He thought for a little, then said, "I don't want to change." This man heard the word of God and believed it. He simply did not want to change his life.

He had completed the first two steps toward becoming a Christian: 1. **Hearing** the word of God: *"So then faith comes by hearing, and hearing by the word of God"* (**Romans 10:17**).
2. **Believing** the word of God: *"But without faith it is impossible to please Him, for he who comes to God must believe that He is, and that He is a rewarder of those who diligently seek Him"* (**Hebrews 11:6**).

When he heard and understood the **third step – repentance**, he did not want to take that step. 3. **Repenting** of past sins and turning away from them. *"Truly, these times of ignorance God overlooked, but now commands all men everywhere to repent"* (**Acts 17:30**).

The third step is necessary. Sins of people separate them from their God. *"Behold, the LORD's hand is not shortened, that it cannot save; nor His ear heavy, that it cannot hear. But your iniquities have separated you from your God; and your sins have hidden His face from you, so that He will not hear"* (**Isaiah 59:1-2**). Without repentance on the part of the person, God does not grant forgiveness. God certainly wants to forgive people. It is stated in **2 Peter 3:9** that God does not want anyone to perish, but he wants all to come to repentance. It is very simple -- sin and God will not dwell in the same person. As an example, dark and light

"Words of Encouragement & Exhortation – 2011"   Curry

do not dwell together.

The fourth step to becoming a Christian is confessing that Jesus is God's Son. This confession is made before one is baptized for the remission of sins. We have an example in **Acts 8**. When the eunuch requested baptism, Philip did not know if the eunuch believed. Here are a few verses of that account (**Acts 8:35-37**): *"Then Philip opened his mouth, and beginning at this Scripture, preached Jesus to him. Now as they went down the road, they came to some water. And the eunuch said, 'See, here is water. What hinders me from being baptized?' Then Philip said, 'If you believe with all your heart, you may.' And he answered and said, 'I believe that Jesus Christ is the Son of God."*

There were people in the first century who would not confess Jesus because of peer pressure. Being a Christian was not popular. In fact, many Christians were put into prison or killed. **If we will not confess Jesus before men, then he will deny us before God (Matthew 10:32-33).**

The fifth and final step to becoming a Christian is to be baptized for the remission of sins. *"Then Peter said to them, 'Repent, and let every one of you be baptized in the name of Jesus Christ for the remission of sins; and you shall receive the gift of the Holy Spirit"* (**Acts 2:38**).

There are two more passages I wish for you to consider with baptism: *"Go therefore and make disciples of all the nations, baptizing them in the name of the Father and of the Son and of the Holy Spirit"* (**Matt 28:19**), and *"Or do you not know that as many of us as were baptized into Christ Jesus were baptized into His death? Therefore we were buried with Him through baptism into death, that just as Christ was raised from the dead by the glory of the Father, even so we also should walk in newness of life"* (**Romans 6:3-4**).

Christians must remain faithful to God (**Revelations 2:10**).

Love, Vernon   *09-18-11*

Salvation or Service ~

What is the goal of your being a Christian? I can think of two reasons: salvation and service.
Every Christian I know wants to go to heaven. I preach *"won't it be wonderful to hear the Lord say, 'Enter into the joy of your lord.'"* Paul said all the persecution on earth did not compare with the glory which shall be revealed! We sing the song, *"Heaven will surely be worth it all."* Salvation!

I preach *"Jesus came to seek and save the lost"!* I preach you must: **hear** the word of God. **Believe** the word. **Repent** of your sins. **Confess** Jesus as God's Son. Be **baptized** for the remission of sins. All these are true facts from the Bible. **When we have obeyed these commands we are saved by the grace of God! Salvation!**

I preach we must worship God according to the commands of God; **sing** songs of praise to God and exhortation to each other. **Pray** to God through Jesus our advocate. **Partake** of the Lord's Supper. **Teach** the word of God. **Give** as we have been prospered and purposed in our hearts to give. All these are facts from the Bible. Salvation!

I preach we must live godly lives putting away sin from ourselves. When a Christian sins, he/she must repent and pray to God for forgiveness. All these are facts from the Bible. Salvation!

I preach service – work. In the parable of the vineyard in **Matthew chapter 20**, Jesus said the workers were hired to be laborers in the vineyard. You understand that when you hire someone, you expect them to work. Idle workers are not paid by you. You have the right to expect those whom you hire to do a job, to work at doing the job. All these are facts from the Bible. Service!

I preach service – work. In **Ephesians chapter 2,** we learn

"Words of Encouragement & Exhortation – 2011"   Curry

about salvation by grace. We also learn about works. **Christians are created for good works!** Are Christians created for salvation or service? Eternal life is a gift from God (**Romans 6:23**). We know obedience is necessary (**Matthew 7:21-23**). So you become a Christian to inherit eternal life! Salvation! God commands Christians to be servants.

Notice these verses:

Romans 6:22: *"But now having been set free from sin, and having become slaves of God, you have your fruit to holiness, and the end, everlasting life".*

Galatians 1:10: *"For do I now persuade men, or God? Or do I seek to please men? For if I still pleased men, I would not be a bondservant of Christ."*

Romans 6:16: *"Do you not know that to whom you present yourselves slaves to obey, you are that one's slaves whom you obey, whether of sin leading to death, or of obedience leading to righteousness?"*

Obedience is complying with God's commands. Many of the commands deal with our relationship with our fellow man.

Matt 20:27-28: *"27 And whoever desires to be first among you, let him be your slave-- 28 just as the Son of Man did not come to be served, but to serve, and to give His life a ransom for many."*

Jesus' obedience to God was fulfilled in giving his life for mankind. Service! Jesus came to do the will of the Father in Heaven. He is described in **Acts 10:38** as he *"who went about doing good and healing all who were oppressed by the devil, for God was with Him."* Did Jesus receive eternal life when his life on earth ended? Yes! Will Christians receive eternal life when this life is over? Yes! **Will those who are NOT servants of God receive eternal life? NO!**

Those who obey the gospel (become a Christian) and sit idle while life goes by will not receive salvation. *We must work the work of God while we are here on earth. Live your life as a servant!* ***Love, Vernon***   *09-25-11*

Fear of the Lord ~

There have been many people who have taught, "Love the Lord". I have heard people say, "We should not fear the Lord." The idea is taught that God is a God of love. Some even believe the God of the Old Testament is different from the God of the New Testament.
Look at these verses in the Old Testament:
Proverbs 1:7:
"The fear of the LORD is the beginning of knowledge, But fools despise wisdom and instruction."
Job 28:28:
"And to man He said, 'Behold, the fear of the Lord, that is wisdom, And to depart from evil is understanding.'"
Psalms 111:10:
"The fear of the LORD is the beginning of wisdom; A good understanding have all those who do His commandments. His praise endures forever."
Psalms 112:1:
"Praise the LORD! Blessed is the man who fears the LORD, who delights greatly in His commandments."
Proverbs 9:10:
"The fear of the LORD is the beginning of wisdom, and the knowledge of the Holy One is understanding."
Ecclesiastes 12:13:
"Let us hear the conclusion of the whole matter: Fear God and keep His commandments, for this is man's all."
Now, if the God of the Old and New Testament are the same, then these verses are truths which would be for us, as well as for Israel. **Was God a God of love in the Old Testament? There are twenty-nine verses in Psalms which refer to God's loving kindness! God taught Israel to love him and each other. There**

are fourteen verses in the Old Testament which say "Love the Lord".

Many times the passage will show the meaning of fear the Lord is to respect him. Let us look at the same idea in the New Testament.

Matthew 10:28:
"And do not fear those who kill the body but cannot kill the soul. But rather fear Him who is able to destroy both soul and body in hell."

Luke 1:50:
"And His mercy is on those who fear Him from generation to generation."

Luke 12:5:
"But I will show you whom you should fear: Fear Him who, after He has killed, has power to cast into hell; yes, I say to you, fear Him!"

Revelation 19:5:
"Then a voice came from the throne, saying, "Praise our God, all you His servants and those who fear Him, both small and great!"

It seems these Scriptures teach respect for the Lord. Then some of the verses teach fear of the Lord in the sense of being afraid of him or at least fear of him because of the consequence of sin.

The Love of God is taught in the New Testament. The whole reason for Jesus coming was to show us how much God loves us. Israel was told over and over of God's love for them.

God loves you with an everlasting love! Do you love him?

1 John 2:5:
"But whoever keeps His word, truly the love of God is perfected in him. By this we know that we are in Him."

The love of God is extended to all mankind. Some do not care! Many do not know! Those who obey him make his love perfect. They also are made perfect by that obedient love.

God bless you!
Love, Vernon   *10-02-11*

Resurrection ~

"Do not marvel at this; for the hour is coming in which all who are in the graves will hear His voice and come forth--those who have done good, to the resurrection of life, and those who have done evil, to the resurrection of condemnation" (**John 5:28-29**).

There are many appointments that are missed by people for various reasons. One reason is they just don't want to keep that appointment. **The resurrection is one of those that no one will have a choice but to keep. All who are in the grave will come forth.** There are a large number of people in the grave. Graves are scattered around the world! During the westward travels in the USA, people died and were buried by their friends along the way. These graves are unknown to this generation. The Lord knows all the dead, just as he knows all the living. None will be overlooked. The first person we have record of dying was Abel. He will be raised from the dead. Peter is dead. He will be raised.

The evil will be raised. Herod the Great will be raised from the dead. Hitler will be raised from the dead. Cain will be raised from the dead. Those who do not know God and do not obey the gospel will be raised from the dead.

Those who are raised will be divided from one another. The evil will be condemned to eternal punishment. **Matthew 25:41, 46 41:** *"Then He will also say to those on the left hand, 'Depart from Me, you cursed, into the everlasting fire prepared for the devil and his angels:"* 46 *"And these will go away into everlasting punishment, but the righteous into eternal life."*

Hell is prepared for the devil and his angels. Those who are lost will spend eternity in hell with the devil and his angels. Notice in **verse 46** above that eternal life and everlasting punishment are both equal in duration. Some teach that hell is temporary. They then

"Words of Encouragement & Exhortation – 2011"   Curry

believe and teach that heaven is eternal. The Lord will find you when it is time for the resurrection. He will not overlook you. He will not make a mistake in his judgment. He will know if you are lost or saved – no appeal.

Paul teaches, in **1 Corinthians 15,** in detail about the resurrection. Some were teaching the resurrection had passed. Some today are teaching the same thing! People do not change! He uses as the prime example the resurrection of Jesus -- *"and that He was buried, and that He rose again the third day according to the Scriptures, and that He was seen by Cephas, then by the twelve. After that He was seen by over five hundred brethren at once, of whom the greater part remain to the present, but some have fallen asleep. After that He was seen by James, then by all the apostles. 8 Then last of all He was seen by me also, as by one born out of due time"* (**1 Corinthians 15:4-8**). Just these few verses show beyond any doubt that Jesus was raised from the dead! Read all of **Chapter 15** about the resurrection.

Jesus was resurrected and we have faith that we will be also! *"Therefore we were buried with Him through baptism into death, that just as Christ was raised from the dead by the glory of the Father, even so we also should walk in newness of life. For if we have been united together in the likeness of His death, certainly we also shall be in the likeness of His resurrection"* (**Romans 6:4-5**).

The resurrection will be a great event for those who are faithful Christians! When we are raised, then we will be judged. After the judgment we will spend eternity with God, Jesus, the Holy Spirit, all the heavenly hosts, and all the saved from the beginning until the end! When Jesus returns, every eye will see him. His followers will rejoice forever! The sinners will weep forever! Are you ready?

Love, Vernon
10-09-11

Quarrels ~

Quarrels do happen -- some between people -- some between animals. It is so hard to keep out of a quarrel which is not our own! I have been told that police do not want to go to the scene of a quarrel between family members. Many times when people try to help stop a quarrel which does not concern them, they get into trouble from both sides! *"He who passes by and meddles in a quarrel not his own is like one who takes a dog by the ears"* (**Proverbs 26:17**). Have you ever taken a dog by the ears? Dogs don't like that!

When is the last time you were involved in a quarrel? It takes two people to quarrel! If you are not willing to quarrel with another then the quarrel will not happen! Do you quarrel with your spouse? Do you wish the quarreling would stop? Then it is your turn to stop quarreling! **Many of the things which couples quarrel about are not really important!** Oh, I know you are right, so what. If you wish the quarreling would stop, then you stop! It takes two.

Who was the last person you quarreled with? Many may answer that it was a family member. I am going to change the tone of this article here and write about myself. I really don't know why you quarrel. I think my reasons for quarreling are; someone has hurt my feelings or I have not gotten my way. You see, I might think at the time that I am tired. Or, I am doing too much; more than my share. Or, the other person doesn't understand me. Those things are just excuses which are not real.

I will try to hurt those who hurt me! That isn't the way of Christ! He tells us to overcome evil with good. *"Do not be overcome by evil, but overcome evil with good"* (**Romans 12:21**). Trying to hurt those who hurt us is of the devil! I think I am just ordinary. I believe many of you react the same way. I must change! What about you?

<u>I want to do things my way! Sometimes my way may hurt others or cause them more work</u> – what do I care? I want my way! Some children grow up having their own way. Most of them have become adults who still want their own way. Should it be my way? I am not talking about spiritual life. It must always be God's way. Have I become a servant to my family? Am I the one who is to submit to their wishes? I could be the leader! Then others must follow me and my way.

The twelve disciples of Jesus quarreled. *"Then a dispute arose among them as to which of them would be greatest"* (**Luke 9:46**). *"Now there was also a dispute among them, as to which of them should be considered the greatest"* (**Luke 22:24**). Jesus knew why they were quarreling. He knows why I am also! Was Jesus thrilled that they desired greatness? **Do you remember he said the greatest in the Church is servant of all!** Sounds like I have gotten it backwards from Jesus! Christians are servants to God and fellowman!

<u>I should/must teach the Bible, but should I quarrel about the Bible? Should I quarrel about doing chores around the house? Should I quarrel about helping the needy? I have given this a lot of thought. I conclude that Christians should not quarrel! I am a Christian, therefore I should not quarrel.</u> **Are you a Christian?**

Talking is not always quarreling. Disagreeing is not always quarreling! We must communicate with our fellowman. Think about your approach to life and the disagreements you have. Think about the way you express yourself.

James 1:19-20: *"So then, my beloved brethren, let every man be swift to hear, slow to speak, slow to wrath; for the wrath of man does not produce the righteousness of God."*

Love, Vernon
10-16-11

Working Together ~

There is in **Nehemiah, Chapter Three,** the information about who built which section of the wall which surrounded Jerusalem. There are many names of the people and the ones who helped each one. There were at least 16 groups of people who worked on the wall. We do not know how long the wall was. We do know it took 52 days to rebuild the wall. I believe this was a short time to do the work.

The people were working together. Nehemiah did not go to Jerusalem and try to do all the work by himself! He first looked the situation over and then told the leaders of his plan. They were willing to work with him. The organization was successful for the doing of the work.

There was opposition to the work. Three men in particular are named (Sanballat, Tobiah, and Geshem) who opposed it. They lied to Nehemiah. They lied about Nehemiah. They ridiculed the work. They threatened the workers. Nehemiah and the other workers did not yield to their words or threats. Sometimes part of them worked while the others stood guard. The people who lived outside the walls moved inside for protection. **During the threats the people only took off their clothes for washing. The work went on! They continued to work together.**

In **Chapter 4, verse six,** *"the people had a mind to work."* It is difficult to get people to work who do not have a mind to work. When people have a mind to work and work together, many things can be accomplished.

The church is spoken of as the body of Christ (**Eph 1:22-23**). This illustration shows the church members must be working together. Our physical bodies become sick when one part does not work properly. It is true of the Lord's church as well. You who are members of the church must: 1) have a mind to work and 2) work together. **Where could this congregation be if each person was working for the Lord?** Much of the preaching and teaching in classes is done only to members of the Lord's body, the Church. That isn't bad! We just need to have sinners to teach these lessons to also! The sinners need to be invited by you and me. That is a small part of the work of the body. If one Christian invited one person – that is one. If one hundred Christians invited one person each that is ninety-nine more than the one! It is very easy to see the difference.

When we sing and you don't sing it takes away from the worship. A lady at the nursing home said yes, she wanted a song book to sing with us. She said "I can't sing but I will anyway." I have been told by many people that I can't sing. One song leader even told me "the singing will be better if you don't sing." I sing anyway. The Lord said *"speaking to one another in psalms and hymns and spiritual songs, singing and making melody in your heart to the Lord"* (**Ephesians 5:19**). I want to obey the Lord!

I attend the worship services of the church when the church meets to worship God. The Lord said, *"not forsaking the assembling of ourselves together, as is the manner of some, but exhorting one another, and so much the more as you see the Day approaching"* (**Hebrews 10:25**). I want to obey this command.

In some way, Nehemiah inspired the people to 'have a mind to work'. In some way we must inspire fellow Christians to have a mind to work.

We must inspire each one to work together. We realize that we are just Christian men and women working together, but we are workers together with God. *"We then, as workers together with Him also plead with you not to receive the grace of God in vain"* (**2 Corinthians 6:1**).

Please consider this verse. *"And let us consider one another in order to stir up love and good works"* (**Hebrews 10:24**).

Love, Vernon   *10-23-11*

Fellowship--

We have fellowship with a lot of different people. **Christians have a special fellowship with each other.** We have a fellowship with sinners, but it is different.

We have a form of fellowship with people because we all are made in the image of God. We are the only creatures made in His image. We can enjoy the animals and even plants, but do not have the fellowship which we have with humans. There are many humans we do not have any fellowship with because we do not associate with them.

We have more in common with all who believe in Jesus than with those people who do not believe in Him. Paul asks the question, what does the temple of God have with idols? The answer is nothing. I am writing about the fellowship which fellow Christians have with each other. When we meet a fellow Christian for the first time, we realize we have a fellowship with them.

We are a family! Just as earthly families have friends who are not part of their family, so also the family of God has friends who are not in His family. Christians have the same Father. It is a great privilege to be a child of God. All who are in the family of God receive the spiritual blessings which are in His family.

Some of the spiritual blessings are: adoption by God, freedom from sin, freedom from guilt, privilege of prayer, and redemption through his blood. Christians have the promise of eternal life in heaven with God and all the heavenly beings. Christians will have a spiritual body just as Jesus has now!

Fellowship of Christians is so very important. We receive from each other encouragement and love. Others may not care much for us, but we have a deep love for each other! Attendance at worship services is important to maintain our obedience to God. Assembling together is important also for the fellowship that we enjoy at the assemblies. If we do not talk/fellowship when things

"Words of Encouragement & Exhortation – 2011"   Curry

are good and all are in obedience, then talking when one is disobedient isn't effective.

Many have criticized congregations for not practicing discipline and disfellowshiping. Many congregations cannot because they do not practice fellowship! **When a person in sin has not been a part of your life, you cannot correct them by taking away that which you have not given them.** Many times we believe our attendance only affects us. That certainly isn't true.

Fellowship is talking, sharing our hurts and joys with those whom we love. It is also sharing the hurts and joys of our fellow Christians.

Sometimes I am amazed at the lack of fellowship which Christians have with one another. Can you believe there are people who attend the same worship place for many years, but do not know each other?

One large congregation realized this was true where they met for worship together. The elders decided to divide the congregation among the elders. Each one became well acquainted with their particular group. Then they changed groups until they knew all the members.

It is hard to become acquainted with everyone with whom we worship. I am not very good at doing so. I do try! I challenge you to try also. When you come into the building for worship and you see someone you cannot call by name, then approach them and become acquainted with them!

When you know everyone, and a visitor comes, you will know they are a visitor! Then you must learn only one family's name at a time as the congregation grows.

I believe closer fellowship will help us to grow because we are more involved in each person's life.

Each of us can continue to try to have more fellowship. (I believe we are already trying.)

Love, Vernon   *10-30-11*

Thank You ~

I have noticed some work which has been done around the building. I appreciate all who are doing what they see needs to be done. A few weeks ago the leaves were bagged and taken off from around the building. Recently the shrubs were trimmed. These things plus others which I have not seen being done, help the looks of our meeting place. **There are many people who do work around who do not seek any recognition.** I do appreciate all the work which is done.

I appreciate the people who visit and encourage fellow members. Every Christian is to be involved in the work of the church. We all are working together with God for the success of the Church of Christ around the world and especially in this community.

I thank YOU.

Holidays --

We are always to give God thanks. So just because it is the Thanksgiving holidays, do not neglect to give thanks. God has given Judy and I a good year. We are thankful for his many blessings. Do continue to pray for Judy's health. We are very concerned about her. Hopefully, the therapy will eliminate her headaches. Some days they are so bad she just can't operate. Our children and grandchildren plan to come for the holidays. We are looking forward to seeing them all.

"Words of Encouragement & Exhortation – 2011"   Curry

Bible Reading ~

Listen to God as he instructs you through His word, the Bible. He tells how salvation has come to all mankind. All who hear the word of God, believe, and obey it, will be saved. He does not exclude any from having salvation. Jesus said, *"Blessed are those who hear the word of God and keep it!"* (**Luke 11:28**). He also says, *"Come to Me, all you who labor and are heavy laden, and I will give you rest"* (**Matthew 11:28**). When he says 'all you' he has included you and all the rest of the world! Read the Bible so you will know the instructions of God.

Prayer --

You as a Christian have the privilege to talk to God anytime you choose. He is your father who lives in heaven. He is able to take care of you and all the things which you worry about. **He requires obedience to him for you to receive all spiritual blessings.** Talk to God everyday. He really does care about you and all your life.

You know that God cannot and will not do anything which is against His will. So we should not ask for wrong things.

Love --

We must love God above all others and love others as much as we love ourselves.

Love, Vernon   *11-20-13*

What Is So Hard?

I hear people say it is really hard to live a Christian life. I wonder what is hard.

I disappoint myself every day. I do or say things which I should not say or do. Do I fail because it is hard to live a Christian life? Think with me about talking and doing.

<u>We are told by God how to talk.</u> *"Let your speech always be with grace, seasoned with salt, that you may know how you ought to answer each one"* (**Colossians 4:6**). As I study this verse I really can't see any reason why I do not obey this verse. It seems that my speech may be connected with my self-control.

<u>I understand by the next verse that self-control is very important.</u> *"Now as he reasoned about righteousness, self-control, and the judgment to come, Felix was afraid and answered, "Go away for now; when I have a convenient time I will call for you"* (**Acts 24:25**). <u>**God put self-control in this verse between righteousness and judgment to come. I must learn to have self-control in every aspect of my life.**</u> When I am talking, I must have control of my thoughts and my tongue. I wish I could be perfect in my speech, then I could be perfect in other aspects of my life. *"For we all stumble in many things. If anyone does not stumble in word, he is a perfect man, able also to bridle the whole body"* (**James 3:2**).

I lie before I think about what I am saying. I do not make up lies. I just do it on the spur of the moment. Do you lie – little white ones are as bad as big black ones. I heard one man say about another man, "He will lie when the truth would fit better." The truth always fits better! *"For which I was appointed a preacher and an apostle-- I am speaking the truth in Christ and not lying--a teacher of the Gentiles in faith and truth"* (**1 Timothy 2:7**)

<u>**Lying is not telling the truth!**</u> When I neglect to teach the truth, then I am lying! So back to the question, "What is so hard about

living a Christian life?" Oh, a couple more verses about talking. *"If anyone among you thinks he is religious, and does not bridle his tongue but deceives his own heart, this one's religion is useless"* (**James 1:26**). *"So then, my beloved brethren, let every man be swift to hear, slow to speak, slow to wrath; for the wrath of man does not produce the righteousness of God"* (**James 1:19-20**).

Maybe it is hard for me to love all people. I sometimes lie to myself and say, "I love them, but I can't stand them!" So maybe I lie because I don't love. If I do not love the people I can see, how can I love the God I cannot see?" *"If someone says, "I love God," and hates his brother, he is a liar; for he who does not love his brother whom he has seen, how can he love God whom he has not seen? And this commandment we have from Him: that he who loves God must love his brother also"* (**1 John 4:20-21**). Is it really hard to obey God if I really love him? He said to love your brother! So why do I find that hard to do? Is it because I really don't love God either?

Is it hard to live a Christian life because I must give as God commands? I must learn to think about what God has given me and it will become easy for me to give to Him!

Is it hard to live a Christian life because God commands me to worship Him? If I really put God first in my life, then it is a joy to meet with people of "like faith" (**2 Peter 1:1**).

When I bring my will in subjection to God's will, I will find living a Christian life becomes easy instead of hard. I must study His Bible and practice being like Him so I can live right. When I live right, I can bring others to God.

This article is written in first person singular. Reread it as if you are the author.

Love, Vernon
11-27-11

Two Sparrows ~

"Are not two sparrows sold for a copper coin? And not one of them falls to the ground apart from your Father's will. But the very hairs of your head are all numbered. Do not fear therefore; you are of more value than many sparrows" (**Matthew 10:29-31**).
I enjoy watching the birds around the feeder in the winter. Recently I saw many different kinds of birds eating. Each species is a little different. I suppose in some little way each bird is different. God is aware of all these birds. He takes care of them. He cares for them. The verses above show God's infinite knowledge and power. He knows about each sparrow. You are much more valuable that a sparrow.

Christmas time in America has become a time for gift-giving. Some people do not receive any gifts. This may cause them to question their value. The value of an individual is not dependent on the gift received from another person. We do not seek the praise of men more than the praise of God.

God has given each of us a gift – His Son's life. God has provided for you – physically and spiritually. You have many physical blessings to be thankful for. God has blessed you with ALL spiritual blessings which are in Christ.

Just as God feeds you, He also gives forgiveness and the promise of eternal life. People many times look at their lives as failures, because of the treatment they receive from other people. You must remember how much God loves you! You must remember how many presents God has given you!

There is nothing which happens to you which God does not know. You have no need which God does not know. Watch the birds -- God takes care of them. He will take care of you also -- be of good cheer.

What Matters --

"But keeping the commandments of God is what matters" (**1 Corinthians 7:19**).
People strive for many things in life. We must remember that all material things will stay in the world. We will die and leave this world, but our earthly possessions will remain here for someone else. That is the reason we are told *'lay up treasures in heaven'*. When your heart is on worldly possessions, you have only earthly treasures. Does it really matter if we have a nicer house than the neighbors?

Remember the man who had many possessions, but God called him a fool because he was going to die that night (**Luke 12:20**)? Another man came to Jesus asking what to do to inherit eternal life. Jesus told him to sell all he had and give it to the poor and follow Jesus. The man went away sorrowful, because he had great possessions (**Mark 10:17-22**).

Solomon searched for what matters. He wrote the book of **Ecclesiastes** about his search. He tried so many different things. In the end he said, *"Let us hear the conclusion of the whole matter: Fear God and keep His commandments, for this is man's all. For God will bring every work into judgment, including every secret thing, whether good or evil"* (**Ecclesiastes 12:13-14**). Many people do not believe this conclusion. Sadly, some Christians have not grasped this understanding either. Each of us will do well to remember – you cannot serve two masters (**Matthew 6:24**). So we must seek the kingdom of God and his righteousness (**Matthew 6:33**).

Jesus said, *"If you love Me, keep My commandments"* (**John 14:15**).

Love, Vernon   *12-04-11*

Is It A State of Mind?

How is everything in your life? Then the questions arise – what does a person judge by? Should we judge ourselves by other people? There is always someone who has more than we do. Does that make our life bad? There are always some who have less than we do. Does that make our life good? Are we content with our lives? Others may not be, but how do you think of yourself? *"Therefore I say to you, do not worry about your life, what you will eat or what you will drink; nor about your body, what you will put on. Is not life more than food and the body more than clothing?"* (**Matthew 6:25**).

How is your health? Many people have failing health. Does that make your life bad? Should we judge ourselves by the people who are less healthy than we? Does that make our lives good? We must know that few, if any, people have perfect health. Is our health good or bad according to our own thinking? *"Which of you by worrying can add one cubit to his stature"* (**Matthew 6:27**)?

How is your spiritual life? Should we compare ourselves with those who are weak/strong? Does that indicate our acceptableness to God? We can learn more about God every day. We can conform ourselves to His will more fully each day. The good or bad of others has nothing to do with our acceptableness to God. We will be judged of the things we have done. We will be judged according to His Word, not compared with others! *"For we dare not class ourselves or compare ourselves with those who commend themselves. But they, measuring themselves by themselves, and comparing themselves among themselves, are not wise"* (**2 Corinthians 10:12**).

Why do some people think their lives good while others are made a wreck by their lives? We must learn to believe in God. Notice this

"Words of Encouragement & Exhortation – 2011"   Curry

verse: *"But without faith it is impossible to please Him, for he who comes to God must believe that He is, and that He is a rewarder of those who diligently seek Him"* (**Hebrews 11:6**). When we believe God, we will rely upon his promises being fulfilled. I understand that you believe he will give the righteous a home in heaven. Do you believe that he will give you food and clothing? *"Therefore do not worry, saying, 'What shall we eat?' or 'What shall we drink?' or 'What shall we wear?' "For after all these things the Gentiles seek. For your heavenly Father knows that you need all these things. But seek first the kingdom of God and His righteousness, and all these things shall be added to you"* (**Matthew 6:31-33**).

It is easy to say that we believe God will reward us with a home in heaven. We can't see heaven. We can't provide heaven for our own home. On the other hand, we can see the earth and the food, houses and all physical things. We tend to trust in ourselves for these material things instead of trusting in God for these things.

Have you really given your trust to God? Are you anxious about material things? I have heard the idea that God helps those who help themselves. That may be based on the verse which states if a man will not work then he should not eat. This past summer many people had gardens or crops which produced very little. They worked. The produce just wasn't there. We must keep in mind that God is the one who gives the increase.

So it is in the spiritual life also. **We must plant the seed (the Word of God). We must baptize in water. It is God who gives the increase.** We do not have the ability to give the increase.

Look at your life. Are you following God? Then your life is good. God bless us as we work for him. He will give the increase.

Love, Vernon
12-11-11

Frigidaire

Frigidaire is a name brand of air-conditioners and they also made refrigerators. I know nothing about them personally so I cannot recommend them. I usually think any product which has been around for years must have some value. You know that may or may not be true of any product.

Neither Air-conditioners or Refrigerators are found in the Bible. There are many things taught as religious beliefs which are not in the Bible either! *Eternal security* or *once saved always saved* is a subject which is not taught in the Bible. In fact, Paul refutes this doctrine in **1 Corinthians 9:27**: *"But I discipline my body and bring it into subjection, lest, when I have preached to others, I myself should become disqualified."*

Many times when those who teach this doctrine have a church member who goes back into sin, they will say, "They never were saved or they could not have left the Lord." Paul said there was a danger of his becoming disqualified. You can't disagree with him. You can't say he wasn't saved. You *can* say he could have been lost had he chosen to leave the Lord!

Some are teaching that it is pleasing to God if we take the Lord's Supper on Saturday or Thursday or on special occasions such as "holy days". The only example of the church partaking of the Lord's Supper is on the first day of the week (Sunday). All of the secular writings concerning the Church partaking of the Lord's Supper affirm the early church met on the first day of the week for that purpose.

Some are teaching that baptism is given to people who are saved. They say that baptism has nothing to do with salvation. Peter records that baptism now saves us, just as Noah was saved by the flood.

"Words of Encouragement & Exhortation – 2011"   Curry

There is a story: Once there was a preacher who invited a man to attend worship. The man answered "peanut butter". The preacher not wanting to show his ignorance just drove off. Then his curiosity got the best of him so he returned and asked the man what he meant by "peanut butter". The man responded, "I don't intend to come to church. Peanut butter is as good as any excuse I could make up." So *Frigidaire* may as well be taught in church as any false doctrine.

Read your Bible so you will know the truth. Jesus said, *"You shall know the truth and the truth will make you free."* We are encouraged to search the scriptures and know what is right. *"Beloved, do not believe every spirit, but test the spirits, whether they are of God; because many false prophets have gone out into the world"* (**1 John 4:1**). *"Test all things; hold fast what is good"* (**1 Thessalonians 5:21**). *"These were more fair-minded than those in Thessalonica, in that they received the word with all readiness, and searched the Scriptures daily to find out whether these things were so"* (**Acts 17:11**).

Love, Vernon
12-18-11

Paper ~

Paper has been around a long time. It is interesting that paper money in the USA isn't made from paper. Paper has been made from various plants and other things through the years. Paper isn't nearly as important as what is written on the paper.

Sadly enough, much paper is used for sinful purposes. Just as the internet, radio and television is sometimes used for evil, paper is also used for evil. We, as readers, must choose what we will read or not read. Some paper should be burned (**Acts 19:19**).

Thankfully, paper is also used to record God's word for us. The paper isn't holy. In fact, the paper which has God's word written on it isn't holy paper. We treat it with respect because of the message which it contains. Remember that Paul asked Timothy, *"Bring the cloak that I left with Carpus at Troas when you come-- and the books, especially the parchments"* (**2 Timothy 4:13**).

Godly people have always respected the word of God – spoken or written. They have always chosen to read and study the Word on a regular basis.

God first gave the Ten Commandments on tablets of stone. Many of the ancient kings had records kept on stone. Stone is harder to carry around than paper. God does refer to the old covenant being written on stone and new covenant being written on our hearts. The Ten Commandments are written in our Bible on paper.

The Jewish people neglected the Old Law. In **2 Chronicles 34**, Hilkiah the priest, while cleaning the temple found the Law of God given through Moses. When he read it to the king, the king tore his clothes. They had wandered far away from the law which God had given to them. The king knew the importance of the law. He called all the leaders of the people together and had the law read to them. Every generation must continue to read and obey the law from God. **We now live under the New Testament, not the Old! It is** equally important that we read and obey the New Testament as the Jewish people should have the Old Testament. Most of our Bibles contain both the Old and New Testaments. The Bibles are not heavy because they are written on paper. We are blessed in America to have the money needed to buy a Bible whenever we need one. The sixty-six books of the Bible are put in the same order in each Bible. The paper and the print are very durable.

We must read the Bible with care – understanding aright the word of God (**2 Timothy 2:15**). Yes, there are places which are hard to understand. Some people wrestle these to their ruin (**2 Peter 3:16**). The Bible was given for the good of mankind. *"And that from childhood you have known the Holy Scriptures, which are able to make you wise for salvation through faith which is in Christ Jesus"* (**2 Timothy 3:15**)

We must study the scriptures. They teach us about God, Jesus, the Holy Spirit, righteousness, sin, eternal damnation and eternal life. On the paper in the Holy Bible we can learn: where we came from; why we are here; where we are going; and the way we are to live while here so we can live in heaven with God eternally.

You may underline a passage on the paper of the Bible. You may make a note to remind you about its meaning. I encourage you to use your Bible regularly to guide your life. The Bible has been proven to be truthful and the inspired Word from God. The Bible is given to us by God. He loved us enough to provide instructions for us to please him in every aspect of our lives.

I own many books totaling thousands of pages, but they are useful to me only if I read them. It is true of the Bible, song books, or any good book. I wonder if paper will become obsolete. I am writing about paper on an electrical machine.

Love, Vernon
12-25-11

Closing Thoughts

As I leave you, dear reader, I close this book of 2011 Bulletin Articles from the Highland Church of Christ, with the following thoughts and Scripture:

The Lord Jesus was asked by a lawyer which is the great commandment, and our Lord replied:

"Thou shalt love the Lord thy God with all thy heart, with all thy soul, and with all thy mind. This is the first and great commandment. And, the second is like unto it, Thou shalt love thy neighbor as thyself" (Matthew 22:35-39).

I pray that you will take the words of Jesus our Lord and Saviour
Close to your heart,
Study your Bible,
Obey its commands,
And resolve to live ever close to the Lord!

In Christian love,
Vernon Curry